9-1-88

Dearest Mother and
+ Dad and Mo

May the rest of lives be
a joyous and Day 1.

Love,
Ruth Shumway
(Eldest Daughter)

LOVE

Ezra Taft Benson
Gordon B. Hinckley
Boyd K. Packer
Marvin J. Ashton
James E. Faust

LOVE

Marion D. Hanks
Jack H. Goaslind
Robert L. Backman
Theodore M. Burton
Loren C. Dunn
Rex D. Pinegar
Robert E. Wells
James M. Paramore
F. Enzio Busche
Yoshihiko Kikuchi
Ronald E. Poelman
H. Burke Peterson
J. Richard Clarke

Deseret Book Company
Salt Lake City, Utah

Original articles from which these chapters have been
adapted, © by Corporation of the President, The Church
of Jesus Christ of Latter-day Saints. Reprinted by permission.
Love is not an official publication of the Church.

First printing September 1986
Second printing December 1986
Third printing March 1987

Library of Congress Cataloging-in-Publication Data

Love.

    Includes index.
    1. Love—Religious aspects—Mormon Church.
2. Mormon Church—Doctrines. 3. Church of Jesus Christ
of Latter-day Saints—Doctrines. I. Benson, Ezra Taft.
BV4639.L66 1986   241'.4   86-16750
ISBN 0-87579-059-3

CONTENTS

A new commandment I give unto you,
That ye love one another;
as I have loved you, that ye also
love one another.
By this shall all men know
that ye are my disciples,
if ye have love one to another.

John 13:34-35

President Ezra Taft Benson

LOVE AND STABILITY IN OUR HOMES

Marriage is the rock foundation, the cornerstone, of civilization. No nation will ever rise above its homes. Marriage and family life are ordained of God. In an eternal sense, salvation is a family affair. God holds parents responsible for their stewardship in rearing their family. It is a most sacred responsibility.

Today we are aware of great problems in our society. The most obvious are sexual promiscuity, homosexuality, drug abuse, alcoholism, vandalism, pornography, and violence. These grave problems are symptoms of failure in the home— the disregarding of principles and practices established by God in the very beginning.

Because parents have departed from the principles the Lord gave for happiness and success, families throughout the world are undergoing great stress and trauma. Many parents have been enticed to abandon their responsibilities in the home to seek after an elusive "self-fulfillment." Some have abdicated parental responsibilities for pursuit of material things, unwilling to postpone personal gratification in the interest of their children's welfare.

It is time to awaken to the fact that there are deliberate efforts to restructure the family along the lines of humanistic values. Images of the family and of love as depicted in television and film often portray a philosophy contrary to the commandments of God.

If one doubts that the family as an institution is being restructured, consider these facts: Nearly one out of every three marriages ends in divorce. The traditional family—one that has a husband, a wife not working outside the home, and children—constitutes less than 15 percent of American households. Approximately 50 percent of the work force is now female. About 56 percent of these female workers are mothers with preschool children, and nearly 60 percent of them have teenagers at home. In the United States alone, it is estimated that eight to ten million youngsters, six and under, are in child-care situations outside the home. Almost one-fifth of all children in the United States live in one-parent homes. No society will long survive without mothers who care for their young and provide that nurturing care so essential for their normal development.

Innocent-sounding phrases are now used to give approval to sinful practices. Thus, the term "alternative life-style" is used to justify adultery and homosexuality, "freedom of choice" to justify abortion, "meaningful relationship" and "self-fulfillment" to justify sex outside of marriage. If we continue with present trends, we can expect to have more emotionally disturbed young people, more divorce, more depression, and more suicide.

The home is the most effective place to instill lasting values in family members. Where family life is strong and based on principles and practices of the gospel of Jesus Christ, these problems do not as readily appear. My plea is that we return to the God-ordained fundamentals that will ensure love, stability, and happiness in our homes. May I offer three fundamentals to happy, enduring family relationships.

First: *A husband and wife must attain righteous unity and oneness in their goals, desires, and actions.*

Marriage itself must be regarded as a sacred covenant before God. A married couple have an obligation not only to each other, but also to God. He has promised blessings to those who honor that covenant. Fidelity to one's marriage vows is absolutely essential for love, trust, and peace. Adultery is unequivocally condemned by the Lord.

Husbands and wives who love each other will find that love and loyalty are reciprocated. This love will provide a nurturing atmosphere for the emotional growth of children. Family life should be a time of happiness and joy that children can look back on with fond memories and associations.

Hear these simple admonitions from the Lord that may be applied to the marriage covenant: "See that ye love one another; cease to be covetous; learn to impart one to another as the gospel requires. . . . Cease to be unclean; cease to find fault one with another." (D&C 88:123-24.) "Thou shalt love thy wife with all thy heart, and shalt cleave unto her and none else. . . . Thou shalt not commit adultery." (D&C 42:22, 24.) "He that hath the spirit of contention is not of me, but is of the devil, who is the father of contention." (3 Nephi 11:29.) And there are many more scriptural admonitions.

Restraint and self-control must be ruling principles in the marriage relationship. Couples must learn to bridle their tongues as well as their passions. Prayer in the home and prayer with each other will strengthen your union. Gradually the thoughts, aspirations, and ideas of each of you will merge into a oneness until you are seeking the same purposes and goals.

Rely on the Lord, the teachings of the prophets, and the scriptures for guidance and help, particularly when there may be disagreements and problems. Spiritual growth comes by solving problems together—not by running from them. Today's inordinate emphasis on individualism brings egotism and separation. Two individuals becoming "one flesh" is still the Lord's standard. (See Genesis 2:24.)

The secret of a happy marriage is to serve God and each other. The goal of marriage is unity and oneness, as well as self-development. Paradoxically, the more we serve one another, the greater is our spiritual and emotional growth.

The first fundamental, then, is to work toward righteous unity.

Second: *Nurture your children with love and the admonitions of the Lord.*

Rearing happy, peaceful children is no easy challenge in today's world, but it can be done, and it is being done. Responsible parenthood is the key.

Above all else, children need to know and feel that they are loved, wanted, and appreciated. They need to be assured of this often. Obviously, this is a role parents should fill, and most often the mother can do it best.

Children need to know who they are in the eternal sense of their identity. They need to know they have an eternal Heavenly Father on whom they can rely, to whom they can pray, and from whom they can receive guidance. They need to know whence they came so that their lives will have meaning and purpose.

Children must be taught to pray, to rely on the Lord for guidance, and to express appreciation for the blessings that are theirs. I recall kneeling at the bedsides of our young children, helping them with their prayers.

Children must be taught right from wrong. They can and must learn the commandments of God. They must be taught that it is wrong to steal, lie, cheat, or covet what others have.

Children must be taught to work at home. They should learn there that honest labor develops dignity and self-respect. They should learn the pleasure of work, of doing a job well.

The leisure time of children must be constructively directed to wholesome, positive pursuits. Too much time spent in viewing television can be destructive, and pornography in this medium should not be tolerated. It is estimated that growing children today watch television over twenty-five hours per week.

Communities have a responsibility to assist the family in promoting wholesome entertainment. What a community tolerates will become tomorrow's standard for today's youth.

Families must spend more time together in work and recreation. Family home evenings should be scheduled once a week as a time for recreation, work projects, skits, songs around the piano, games, special refreshments, and family prayers. Like iron links in a chain, this practice will bind a family together in love, pride, tradition, strength, and loyalty.

Family study of the scriptures should be the practice in our homes each Sabbath day. Daily devotionals are also a commendable practice, where scripture reading, singing of hymns, and family prayer are a part of our daily routine.

Third: *Parents must prepare their children for the ordinances of the gospel.*

The most important teachings in the home are spiritual. Parents are commanded to prepare their sons and daughters for the ordinances of the gospel: baptism, confirmation, priesthood ordinations, and temple marriage. They are to teach them to respect and honor the Sabbath day, to keep it holy. Most important, they are to instill within their children a desire for eternal life and to earnestly seek that goal above all else.

Eternal life may be obtained only by obedience to the laws and ordinances of the gospel. When parents themselves have complied with the ordinances of salvation, when they have set the example of a temple marriage, not only is their own marriage more likely to succeed, but their children are far more likely to follow their example.

Parents who provide such a home will have, as the Lord has said, "a house of prayer, a house of fasting, a house of faith, a house of learning, . . . a house of order, a house of God." (D&C 88:119.) Regardless of how modest or humble that home may be, it will have love, happiness, peace, and joy. Children will grow up in righteousness and will desire to serve the Lord.

President Joseph F. Smith gave this counsel to parents: "The home is what needs reforming. Try today, and tomorrow, to make a change in your home by praying twice a day with your family. . . . Ask a blessing upon every meal you eat. Spend ten minutes . . . reading a chapter from the words of the Lord in the [scriptures]. . . . Let love, peace, and the Spirit of the Lord, kindness, charity, sacrifice for others, abound in your families. Banish harsh words, . . . and let the Spirit of God take possession of your hearts. Teach to your children these things, in spirit and power. . . . Not one child in a hundred would go astray, if the home environment, example and training, were in harmony with . . . the gospel of Christ." (*Gospel Doctrine,* Salt Lake City: Deseret Book Co., 1939, p. 302.) I testify that, by following these precepts and practices, serious problems with the family can and will be avoided.

Thank God for the joys of family life. I have often said there can be no genuine happiness separate and apart from a good home. The sweetest influences and associations of life are there. God bless us to strengthen our homes with love and unity and by following his precepts.

Elder Boyd K. Packer

LOVE AND MARRIAGE

The prophet Jacob foretold the destruction of a people because they were blind to ordinary things, "which blindness," he said, "came by looking beyond the mark." (Jacob 4:14.) We often seek for things we cannot seem to find when they are within easy reach—ordinary, obvious things.

I wish to talk about an ordinary word. I have tried for months—really tried—to find some way to hold this word up in such a way that you would be very impressed with what it means. The word is *marriage*. I wish that I could set before you a finely carved chest, placing it where the light is just right. I would carefully unlatch it and reverently uncover the word—*marriage*. Perhaps then you would see that it is priceless!

I cannot show it to you that way, so I will do the best I can using other ordinary words. It is my purpose to endorse and to favor, to encourage, and to defend marriage.

Many regard marriage nowadays as being, at best, semi-precious, and by some it is thought to be worth nothing at all. I have seen and heard, as you have seen and heard, the signals all about us, carefully orchestrated to convince us that marriage is out of date and in the way. There is a practice, now quite prevalent, for unmarried couples to live together, a counterfeit of marriage. They suppose that they shall have all that marriage can offer without the obligations connected with it. They are wrong! However much they hope to find in a relationship of that kind, they will lose more. Living together without marriage destroys something inside all who participate. Virtue, self-esteem, and refinement of character wither away. Claiming that it will not happen does not prevent the loss; and these virtues, once lost, are not easily reclaimed. To suppose that one day they may nonchalantly change their habits and immediately claim all that might have been theirs had they not made a mockery of marriage is to suppose something that will not be. One day, when they come to themselves, they will reap disappointment.

One cannot degrade marriage without tarnishing other words as well, such words as *boy, girl, manhood, womanhood, husband, wife, father, mother, baby, children, family, home*. Such words as *unselfishness* and *sacrifice* will then be tossed aside. Then self-respect will fade and love itself will not want to stay.

If you have been tempted to enter such a relationship or if you now live with another without marriage, leave! Withdraw from it! Run away from it! Do not continue with it! Or, if you can, make a marriage out of it. Even a rickety marriage will serve good purpose as long as two people struggle to keep it from falling down around them.

And now a word of warning. One who destroys a marriage takes upon himself a very great responsibility indeed. *Marriage is sacred.* To willfully destroy a marriage, either your own or that of another couple, is to offend God. Such a thing will not be lightly considered in the judgments of the Almighty, and in the eternal scheme of things it will not easily be forgiven.

Do not threaten nor break up a marriage. Do not translate some disenchantment with your own marriage partner or an attraction for someone else into justification for any conduct that would destroy a marriage. This monumental transgression frequently places heavy burdens upon little children. They do not understand the selfish yearnings of unhappy adults who are willing to buy their own satisfaction at the expense of the innocent.

God himself decreed that the physical expression of love, that union of male and female which has power to generate life, is authorized only in marriage. Marriage is the shelter where families are created. That society which puts low value on marriage sows the wind and, in time, will reap the whirlwind—and thereafter, unless they repent, the members of that society bring upon themselves a holocaust.

Some think that every marriage must expect to end in unhappiness and divorce, with the hopes and dreams predestined to end in a broken, sad wreck of things. Some marriages do bend, and some will break, but we must not, because of this, lose faith in marriage nor become afraid of it. Broken marriages are not typical.

Remember that trouble attracts attention. We travel the highway with thousands of cars moving in either direction without paying much attention to any of them. But should an accident occur, we notice immediately. If it happens again, we get the false impression that no one can go safely down the road. One accident may make the front page, while a hundred million cars that pass safely are not regarded as worth mentioning.

Writers think that a happy, stable marriage does not have the dramatic appeal, the conflict worth featuring in a book or a play or a film. Therefore, we constantly hear about the ruined ones and we lose our perspective.

I believe in marriage. I believe it to be the ideal pattern for human living. I know it to be ordained of God. The restraints relating to it were designed to protect our happiness. I do not know of any better time in all of the history of the world for a young couple who are of age and prepared and who are in love to think of marriage. There is no better time because it is *your* time. I know that these are very troubled times. Troubles like we have now are very hard on marriages.

Do not lose faith in marriage—not even if you have been through the unhappiness of a divorce and are surrounded with pieces of a marriage that has fallen apart. If you have honored your vows and your partner did not do so, remember that God is watching over us. One day, after all of the tomorrows have passed, there will be recompense. Those who have been moral and faithful to their covenants will be happy, and those who have not will be otherwise.

Some marriages have broken up in spite of all that one partner could do to hold the marriage together. While there may be faults on both sides, I do not condemn the innocent one who suffers in spite of all that was desired and done to save the marriage. To you I say, do not lose faith in marriage itself. Do not let your disappointment leave you bitter or cynical or justify any conduct that is unworthy.

If you have had no opportunity for marriage or if you have lost your companion in death, keep your faith in marriage.

Some years ago an associate of mine lost his beloved wife. She died after a lingering illness, and he watched in helpless agony as the doctors withdrew all hope. One day near the end she told him that when she was gone, she wanted him to marry again and he was not to wait too long a time. He protested. The children were nearly grown, and he would go the rest of the way alone. She turned away and wept and said, "Have I been such a failure that after all our years together you would rather go unmarried? Have I been such a failure?" In due time there came another woman, and their life together has reaffirmed his faith in marriage. And I have the feeling that his first beloved wife is deeply grateful to the second one, who filled the place that she could not keep.

Marriage is yet safe, with all its sweet fulfillment, with all its joy and love. In marriage, all of the worthy yearnings of the human soul, all that is physical and emotional and spiritual, can be fulfilled.

Marriage is not without trials of many kinds. These tests forge virtue and strength. The tempering that comes in marriage and family life produces men and women who will someday be exalted.

God has ordained that life should have its beginning within the protecting shelter of marriage, conceived in a consummate expression of love and nurtured and fostered with that deeper love which is accompanied always by sacrifice.

Marriage offers fulfillment all the way through life—in youth and young love, the wedding and on the honeymoon, with the coming of little children and the nurturing of them. Then come the golden years when young ones leave the nest to build a nest of their own. The cycle then repeats itself, as God has decreed it should.

There is another dimension to marriage that we know of in

the Church. It came by revelation. This glorious, supernal truth teaches us that marriage is meant to be eternal. There are covenants we can make if we are willing, and bonds we can seal if we are worthy, that will keep marriage safe and intact beyond the veil of death.

The Lord has declared, "For behold, this is my work and my glory—to bring to pass the immortality and eternal life of man." (Moses 1:39.) The ultimate end of all activity in the Church is that a man and his wife and their children can be happy at home and that the family can continue through eternity. All Christian doctrine is formulated to protect the individual, the home, and the family.

These lines express something of the place of marriage in the eternal progress of man:

> *We have within a burning flame,*
> *A light to kindle lights,*
> *The sacred fire of life itself,*
> *Which if misused ignites*
> *A smold'ring, suffocating cloud*
> *Of sorrow and distress.*
> *When used by law this power brings forth*
> *A life, a family, happiness.*
>
> *Tempters from the darkest realm*
> *Seek to pervert this power*
> *In acts of wickedness and waste*
> *Until there comes the hour*
> *Of judgment and of recompense,*
> *When bitter tears are shed*
> *O'er power once held to foster life*
> *That now is gone and dead.*
>
> *I know this power to be a key,*
> *A very key to God's own plan*
> *Which brings to pass eternal life*
> *And immortality for man.*
> *And marriage is the crucible*
> *Where elements of life combine,*
> *Where mortal temples are conceived*
> *Within that plan divine.*

Then spirit offspring of our God
Can come through mortal birth
To have a choice, to face the test—
The purpose of our stay on earth.
Here good and evil stand alike
Before decision's sovereign nod.
Those who elect the righteous path
Will part the veil, return to God.

A gift from God, the plan provides
That mortal beings in humble strait
Be given power, supernal power,
To share their love and help create
A living child, a living soul,
Image of man, and of Deity.
How we regard this sacred gift
Will fix our course, our destiny!

Eternal love, eternal marriage, eternal increase! This ideal, which is new to many, can, when thoughtfully considered, keep a marriage strong and safe. No relationship has more potential to exalt a man and a woman than the marriage covenant. No obligation in society or in the Church supersedes it in importance.

I thank God for marriage. I thank God for temples. I thank God for the glorious sealing power, that power which transcends all that we have been given, through which our marriages may become eternal.

Elder James E. Faust

BRETHREN, LOVE YOUR WIVES

What should a wife mean to her husband? And how does she deserve to be treated?

No man can become completely adequate or function responsibly without help from others. Of course, too much help or the wrong kind of help stifles and is counterproductive. But at the heart of human adequacy is self-esteem, which is fed by rich, life-giving love, confidence, and caring of others. This support can come richly from family and friends. But for men it comes mostly from their wives.

Consequently, there is no higher commitment for any man than to be loyal to his commitment to God and to his wife and family. The reciprocating fruits from keeping that commitment will usually give him boundless sustaining love and the challenge to reach deep down inside himself to call forth the seeds of the finest of his gifts for their full flowering. He will enjoy a place of honor, dignity, and respect.

Most men worry about succeeding in their life's work and spend much time and effort at their profession. But I've learned that the way to put one's *professional* life in order is to put one's *personal* life in order. How can we be adequate at anything professionally without being adequate as men, husbands, and

13

fathers first? And yet, we often shortchange those who mean most to us, thinking that because of our special training and special knowledge, others have a greater claim on our time and concern than do our own families. I fully recognize that the work my wife has done in my home is more important to me than any work I have done.

The relationship between husband and wife is the linchpin in the whole family relationship. I am sorry that I have come so late to a fuller appreciation of the extent of the needs of our wives and womenfolk for love, appreciation, companionship, and recognition. These needs are great, they are constant, and they need to be met frequently. Kindness and courtesy do not begin in the professional office—they begin at home.

I am also sorry that I have not appreciated sooner the great sublime, unique gifts our wives inherit from divinity. I speak of their womanly intuition and their steadfast faith and capacity to love. Properly nurtured, the eternal relationship of a husband and wife flowers into a love of consummate beauty.

It is an unrighteous exercise of priesthood authority for a man, as a conduit through his priesthood office, to withhold or limit blessings that should flow through the priesthood to his wife and family. Priesthood blessings are not just male- or husband-limited, but reach their potential flowering in the eternal relationship of the husband and the wife sharing and administering these great blessings to the family. Our wives have priesthood blessings, though not priesthood offices. These blessings are the keys to eternal life, salvation, and exaltation through obedience.

Elder Boyd K. Packer recently asked me a very penetrating question: "What would you have been without your wife, Ruth?" I could have answered immediately, "Not much," but he already knew that. I took him seriously and spent the next twenty-four hours thinking about what I would have been without the loving, sweet support and the discipline of Ruth Wright in my life. It shocked me a little to even think about what life would be and would have been without her. I would have to answer honestly that without my wife, I would have been pretty much of a failure. I do not claim to be an expert in marriage: I have only been married once. But, thanks to my good wife, it took. I do not claim to have a better marriage than anyone else, but I do claim to be married to a great companion.

I am still moved by what President Marion G. Romney said to the Twelve in a meeting in the temple a few days after the death of his wife, Sister Ida Romney, which with his permission I share. He said, "When Ida died, something went out of me. The holding force was gone." At the graveside, President Romney counseled me, "Be good to your wife. Take her with you everywhere you can. The time will come when you will not be able to be together."

The most sacred, intimate, and blessed relationship of life is between husband and wife. I do not love anybody as I love my wife. My mother has my father, and my children have their companions, but Ruth is me. Our wives become part of us, and they become like our own flesh—and, as Paul counseled, we should love them as such. (See Ephesians 5:28-33.) The simple truth is that it is not good for man to be alone. The greatest sustaining influence in my mature life has been the constant supporting, unqualified, unreserved love I have felt for my wife. The sacred relationship we have had has been the supreme benediction of my life. I just can't imagine what my life would have been like without that blessing.

Without our wives we would never be privileged to be fathers and grandfathers and to enjoy all the blessings that that entails. This relation has to come first in all of our relationships with other people. It is the thing that helps to fit together all of the parts of the jigsaw puzzle of eternal joy and fulfillment and happiness.

One of the greatest blessings of having a good wife is that she can be the source of the most basic of all human needs— love. The greatest unreserved love that I have received in my life has been from the good women in my family: my wife, my mother, my mother-in-law, my grandmothers, my daughters, and my sweet granddaughters. The example of how to be a man came from others: my father, my grandfather, my uncles, my older brother Gus, and many Church leaders—bishops, stake presidents, and the General Authorities.

If I hadn't married Ruth, I would not have known her mother, Elizabeth Hamilton Wright. She was one of the twenty-

two children of James C. Hamilton, bishop of the Millcreek
Ward in Salt Lake City for over twenty-five years. She went only
as far as the third grade. Because she had a special gift for
teaching children, she was taken out of school to tend and teach
the younger children in the family. It used to break my heart to
see her struggle to write a simple note, but she had spiritual
maturity, wisdom, insight, and faith like my own mother. She
understood things completely by the Holy Spirit. I loved her for
her greatness and goodness and because she taught my wife so
well. And my wife in turn has taught our children and grandchildren.

One of the areas in which our wives perform a very great
service is in their loving discipline of us. In their discipline they
keep us closer to what we ought to be in our holy callings. In
their discipline they teach us. It is part of the polishing we
need to fill in the holes in our character and smooth the rough
edges and make us more adequate. Together we are a team—
we are one.

President N. Eldon Tanner's daughter Isabel said about her
father, "When Mother married Daddy, he was just a farm boy."
But she went on to say that when Sister Tanner would give him
a loving suggestion, unlike many men who bridle or argue
when their wives tell them something that is good for them, he
would simply say, "If you think that's what I should do, I'll do it."
Listening to Sister Tanner and listening to the Lord made a very
great man out of President Tanner.

I am grateful to many of the Brethren for their examples of
kindness and thoughtfulness and solicitude to their wives.
When I was in a stake presidency, Elder S. Dilworth Young of
the First Quorum of the Seventy came to our stake conference.
At the time his wife, Gladys, was an invalid, having suffered
from a cruel stroke. She remained that way for many years.
Brother Young made the extra effort to dress her, feed her, and
care for her. In all my life I have not seen a greater example of
gentleness, kindness, and solicitude than Brother Young
showed to Gladys. It was an example of perfect love. When I
obtained his permission to tell of this, he said, "It was the worst
thing in the world that could have happened to Gladys and the

best thing for me. It made me decent. I learned what love really should be."

Perhaps in these times of great stress, we can become what we ought to be in our relationships with our wives. Perhaps the eternal "every day" causes some of us to be more casual than we ought to be. Of course, we love our wives, but perhaps we take them for granted too much of the time. Perhaps too often we fail to express our appreciation to them in little ways. I know I do. We could certainly show more affection and always look upon our companions with love and respect. We can surely be polite and courteous if we try. We can nourish and cherish them. The simple fact is that few of us could function nearly as well as we do without the support of our gracious and loving wives. They make our homes the heaven on earth that they are. How can I expect God to honor me and be pleased with my service if I do not honor and cherish my very own companion?

In the scriptures we are told that we should not be un-equally yoked together. (See 2 Corinthians 6:14.) I fear that in terms of our total person, our wives perhaps do a better job than we husbands do in being Christlike, thoughtful, kind, gracious, and loving. I feel that Ruth deserves a better me. As Latter-day Saints, we all have the responsibility to be instru-ments in imparting righteousness to the world. Unless we impart a full measure of righteousness to our wives and families, we will be blunted instruments to the rest of the world.

We must strive for greater spirituality in our relationships, and especially in our homes. Literally taking the Lord into partnership with us will bring us a full measure of peace, happiness, unity, and contentment. We need these blessings in our lives in order to be what we ought to be—more adequate vessels for the work we have been commissioned to do. We have the responsibility to bless the lives of others. If our own lives and spiritual batteries are not full and complete, how can we expect to touch the world and bless others?

I know that the gospel is true, and I know that a substantial part of that gospel is how I treat my Ruth on an hour-by-hour, day-by-day, ongoing basis. I believe that none of us can come into full possession of all of our powers without an eternal companion. I suggest that the ultimate judgment will come to every man in terms of what kind of person he has been, what kind of husband he has been, what kind of father he has been, and what kind of family he has raised. Indeed, the Lord has commanded: "Thou shalt love thy wife with all thy heart, and shalt cleave unto her and none else." (D&C 42:22.)

President Gordon B. Hinckley

AND THE GREATEST OF THESE IS LOVE

When I was a little boy, we children traded paper hearts at school on Valentine's Day. At night we dropped them at the doors of our friends, stamping on the porch, and then running in the dark to hide. Almost without exception those valentines had printed on them the words "I love you."

I have since come to know that love is more than a paper heart. Love is of the very essence of life. It is the pot of gold at the end of the rainbow. Yet it is more than the end of the rainbow. Love is at the beginning also, and from it springs the beauty that arches across the sky on a stormy day. Love is the security for which children weep, the yearning of youth, the adhesive that binds marriage, and the lubricant that prevents devastating friction in the home. It is the peace of old age, the sunlight of hope shining through death. How rich are those who enjoy it in their associations with family, friends, church, and neighbors.

I am one who believes that love, like faith, is a gift of God. I agree with the expression, "Love cannot be forced, love cannot be coaxed and teased." (Pearl Buck.)

In our youth, we sometimes acquire faulty ideas of love, believing that it can be imposed or simply created for convenience. I noted the following in a newspaper column:

"One of the grand errors we tend to make when we are young is supposing that a person is a bundle of qualities, and we add up the individual's good and bad qualities, like a bookkeeper working on debits and credits. If the balance is favorable, we may decide to take the jump [into marriage]. . . . The world is full of unhappy men and women who married because . . . it seemed to be a good investment.

"Love, however, is not an investment; it is an adventure. And when marriage turns out to be as dull and comfortable as a sound investment, the disgruntled party soon turns else-where. . . . Ignorant people are always saying, 'I wonder what he sees in her [or him],' not realizing that what he [or she] sees in her [or him] (and what no one else can see) is the secret essence of love." (Sydney J. Harris, *Deseret News.*)

I think of two friends from my high school and university years. One was a boy from a country town, plain in appearance, without money or apparent promise. He had grown up on a farm; and if he had any quality that was attractive, it was the capacity to work. He carried bologna sandwiches in a brown paper bag for his lunch and swept the school floors to pay his tuition. But with all of his rustic appearance, he had a smile and a personality that seemed to sing of goodness. The other was a city girl who had come out of a comfortable home. She would not have won a beauty contest, but she was wholesome in her decency and integrity, and attractive in her decorum and dress.

Something wonderful took place between them. They fell in love. Some whispered that there were far more promising boys for her, and a gossip or two noted that perhaps other girls might have interested him. But these two laughed and danced and studied together through their school years. They married when people wondered how they could ever earn enough to stay alive. He struggled through his professional school and came out well in his class. She scrimped and saved and worked and prayed. She encouraged and sustained, and when things were really tough, she said quietly, "Somehow we can make it." Buoyed by her faith in him, he kept going through these difficult years. Children came, and together they loved them and nourished them and gave them the security that came of their own love for and loyalty to one another. Now many years have passed. Their children are grown, a lasting credit to them, to the Church, and to the communities in which they live.

I remember seeing this couple on a plane as I returned from an assignment. I walked down the aisle in the semi-darkness of the cabin and saw a woman, white-haired, her head on her husband's shoulder as she dozed. His hand was clasped warmly about hers. He was awake and recognized me. She awakened, and we talked. They were returning from a convention where he had delivered a paper before a learned society. He said little about it, but she proudly spoke of the honors accorded him.

I wish that I might have caught with a camera the look on her face as she talked about him. Forty-five years earlier people without understanding had asked what they saw in each other. I thought of that as I returned to my seat on the plane. Their friends of those days saw only a farm boy from the country and a smiling girl with freckles on her nose. But these two found in each other love and loyalty, peace and faith in the future. There was a flowering in them of something divine, planted there by that Father who is our God. In their school days they had lived worthy of that flowering of love. They had lived with virtue and faith, with appreciation and respect for self and one another. In the years of their difficult professional and economic struggles, they had found their greatest earthly strength in their companionship. Now in mature age, they were finding peace and quiet satisfaction together. Beyond all this, they were assured of an eternity of joyful association through priesthood covenants long since made and promises long since given in the House of the Lord.

There are other great and necessary expressions of the gift of love. In Matthew we read:

"Then one of them, which was a lawyer, asked [Jesus] a question, tempting him, and saying, Master, which is the great commandment in the law?

"Jesus said unto him, Thou shalt love the Lord thy God with all thy heart, and with all thy soul, and with all thy mind. This is the first and great commandment. And the second is like unto it, Thou shalt love thy neighbour as thyself. On these two commandments hang all the law and the prophets." (Matthew 22:35-40.)

Who is my neighbor? To answer this, we need only to read the moving parable of the good Samaritan, or the word of the Lord concerning the day of judgment when the King shall "say unto them on his right hand, Come, ye blessed of my Father, inherit the kingdom prepared for you from the foundation of the world; for I was an hungred, and ye gave me meat: I was thirsty, and ye gave me drink: I was a stranger, and ye took me in: naked, and ye clothed me: I was sick, and ye visited me: I was in prison, and ye came unto me.

"Then shall the righteous answer him, saying, Lord, when saw we thee an hungred, and fed thee? or thirsty, and gave thee drink? When saw we thee a stranger, and took thee in? or naked, and clothed thee? Or when saw we thee sick, or in prison, and came unto thee?

"And the King shall answer and say unto them, Verily I say unto you, Inasmuch as ye have done it unto one of the least of these my brethren, ye have done it unto me." (Matthew 25:34-40.)

The greatest challenge we face in our hurried, self-centered lives is to follow this counsel of the Master. Years ago I read the story of a young woman who went into a rural area as a schoolteacher. Among those in her class was a girl who had failed before and who was failing again. The student could not read. She came from a family without means to take her to a larger city for examination to determine whether she had a problem that could be remedied. Sensing that the difficulty might lie with the girl's eyes, the young teacher arranged to take the student, at the teacher's own expense, to have her eyes tested. A deficiency was discovered that could be corrected with glasses. Soon an entire new world opened to the girl. For the first time in her life, she saw clearly the words before her. The salary of that country schoolteacher was meager, but out of the little she had, she made an investment that completely changed the life of a failing student, and in doing so she found a new dimension in her own life.

Every returned missionary can recount experiences of losing oneself in the service of others and finding that to be the most rewarding experience of his or her life. Every member of the Church actively involved in service to God and others can recount similar stories, as can devoted parents and marriage partners who have given of their time and means, who have loved and sacrificed so greatly that their concern for each other and their children has known almost no bounds.

Love is the only force that can erase the differences between people, that can bridge chasms of bitterness. I recall these lines by Edwin Markham:

> *He drew a circle that shut me out—*
> *Heretic, rebel, a thing to flout.*
> *But Love and I had the wit to win:*
> *We drew a circle that took him in.*

He who most beautifully taught this everlasting truth was the Son of God, the one perfect exemplar and teacher of love. His coming to earth was an expression of his Father's love: "For God so loved the world, that he gave his only begotten Son, that whosoever believeth in him should not perish, but have everlasting life. For God sent not his Son into the world to condemn the world; but that the world through him might be saved." (John 3:16-17.)

The Savior spoke prophetically of that sacrifice and of the love that culminated in his redemptive sacrifice when he declared, "Greater love hath no man than this, that a man lay down his life for his friends." (John 15:13.) To all who would be his disciples, he has given the great commandment: "A new commandment I give unto you, That ye love one another; as I have loved you." (John 13:34.)

If the world is to be improved, the process of love must make a change in the hearts of people. It can do so when we look beyond self to give our love to God and others, and when we do so with all our heart, with all our soul, and with all our mind. The Lord has declared in modern revelation, "If your eye be single to my glory, your whole bodies shall be filled with light, and there shall be no darkness in you." (D&C 88:67.)

As we look with love and gratitude to God, as we serve him with an eye single to his glory, there goes from us the darkness of sin, the darkness of selfishness, the darkness of pride. There will come an increased love for our Eternal Father and for his Beloved Son, our Savior and our Redeemer. There will come a greater sense of service toward our fellowmen, less of thinking of self and more of reaching out to others. This principle of love is the basic essence of the gospel of Jesus Christ. Without love of God and love of neighbor, there is little else to commend the gospel to us as a way of life.

Paul the Apostle spoke well these words: "Though I speak with the tongues of men and of angels, and have not [love], I am become as sounding brass, or a tinkling cymbal And though I have the gift of prophecy, and understand all mysteries, and all knowledge; and though I have all faith, so that I could remove mountains, and have not [love], I am nothing. . . . [Love] never faileth: but whether there be tongues, they shall cease; whether there be knowledge, it shall vanish away." (1 Corinthians 13:1-2, 8.)

The Master taught: "For whosoever will save his life shall lose it: but whosoever will lose his life for my sake, the same shall save it." (Luke 9:24.) This remarkable and miraculous process occurs in our own lives as we reach out with love to serve others. Each of us can, with effort, successfully root the principle of love deeply in our being so that we may be nourished by its great power all our lives. For as we tap into the power of love, we will come to understand the great truth written by John: "God is love: and he that dwelleth in love dwelleth in God." (1 John 4:16.)

Elder F. Enzio Busche

THE POWER OF LOVE IN THE FAMILY

There has never been a time in the entire history of mankind when marriage and the institution of the family have been so endangered as in this generation. Nearly all the circumstances that have made family life in the past the most natural way for people to live together have changed—and it has all happened in the brief span of the last seventy years.

Just a little over a generation ago, members of the average family had to work long days to provide a humble living, and the dark evenings found them huddled around a fire, enjoying one another's company in singing and sharing personal experiences. This was the natural way for education and entertainment and was nearly the perfect environment for a harmonious family life.

Today, influences from literally unlimited sources through the media of radio, television, and print, together with numerous inventions of modern civilization, have drastically changed the historical cultural setting of the family. In this time of special challenge for marriage and the family, the Lord has restored, through his prophets in these latter days, the eternal dimension of that sacred covenant between husband and wife and has charged us with a new awareness of the real purpose of the family.

The integrity of this covenant became the center of revealed gospel truths in these latter days, well summarized by the late prophet David O. McKay, who said, "No other success can compensate for failure in the home." It is obvious that in marriage today, we cannot rely merely on patterns of the past without developing, perfecting, and putting into action that power which the Lord has given us as the greatest commandment—the commandment to love one another.

Still, after nearly two thousand years, the people of the world are refusing to accept the words of the Savior found in Matthew: "Ye have heard that it hath been said, Thou shalt love thy neighbour, and hate thine enemy. But I say unto you, Love your enemies, bless them that curse you, do good to them that hate you, and pray for them which despitefully use you, and persecute you." (Matthew 5:43-44.)

This love that Christ is teaching us is not the same as the world's love. It does not mean just to love the one who is nice, who behaves well and is respected, powerful, and influential. Our Heavenly Father, through his prophets, calls us to develop the love of God as a power from above that cannot be threatened through outward circumstances. This love of God, according to the prophet Nephi of the Book of Mormon, has to be achieved and is "the most desirable above all things." (1 Nephi 11:22.)

However, as King Benjamin, another great Book of Mormon leader, teaches us, this love of God will not be in us as long as we remain in our natural state. "The natural man is an enemy to God," he explains. (Mosiah 3:19.) We have to overcome this natural man—this "enemy to God"—our natural self. According to King Benjamin, we have to learn to listen to the enticings of the Holy Spirit and literally make a covenant with God, accepting the atonement of the Savior and becoming as children—submissive, meek, humble, patient, full of love, and willing to submit to all things, even as a child submits to his father. (See Mosiah 3:19.)

What a powerful message, and what a challenging responsibility! We have to learn to commit ourselves anew every day, and to center our lives around *this*—the key commandment from God to his children.

Moroni, another Book of Mormon prophet, tells us how we can achieve this love: "Charity is the pure love of Christ, and it endureth forever; and whoso is found possessed of it at the last day, it shall be well with him. Wherefore, my beloved brethren, pray unto the Father with all the energy of heart, that ye may be filled with this love, which he hath bestowed upon all who are true followers of his Son, Jesus Christ; that ye may become the sons of God." (Moroni 7:47-48.)

Our Heavenly Father want us to fill ourselves with this love, which is without condition. Filled with this love, we are prepared to receive the admonition to take upon ourselves the cross of our daily lives and, in humility, learn to follow in his footsteps.

A marriage that is built on a foundation of unconditional love in an eternal covenant is the complete antithesis of two self-centered individuals living together, as we often observe in today's society. In the marriage that is built on the cornerstone of unconditional love, which is the love of God, the idea of divorce is unthinkable, and even short separations bring unquenchable pain. Separation and divorce are signs of weakness and sometimes wickedness.

The Lord has given a clear teaching on the sacredness of the marriage covenant. We read in Matthew the words of the Savior to the Pharisees when they asked, "Is it lawful for a man to put away his wife for every cause?"

He responded: "Have ye not read, that he which made them at the beginning made them male and female, and said, For this cause shall a man leave father and mother, and shall cleave to his wife: and they twain shall be one flesh? Wherefore they are no more twain, but one flesh. What therefore God hath joined together, let not man put asunder.

"They say unto him, Why did Moses then command to give a writing of divorcement, and to put her away?

"He saith unto them, Moses *because of the hardness of your hearts* suffered you to put away your wives: but from the beginning it was not so." (Matthew 19:3-8. Italics added.)

The only way that we will not suffer from the hardness of our hearts, as Christ explains, is to build within ourselves the power of love, literally asking our Heavenly Father for this gift, and becoming sanctified through the atonement of Christ. When we become as children in humility, we can be filled with unconditional love and, in this love, we can be in the Spirit and with the Spirit, being directed in all the challenges of our lives.

We know that in our imperfect bodies and in our strivings for perfection, many of us are confronted with situations where members of our own families can behave like enemies. Then the time comes when love as a power is needed and tested, for the person who has earned love the least often needs it most.

One day when circumstances made it necessary for me to be at home at an unusual time, I witnessed from another room how our eleven-year-old son, just returning from school, was directing ugly words toward his younger sister. They were words that offended me—words that I had never thought our son would use. My first reaction in my anger was to get up and go after him. Fortunately, I had to walk across the room and open a door before I could reach him, and in those few seconds I fervently prayed to my Heavenly Father to help me to handle the situation. Peace came over me. I was no longer angry.

My son, being shocked to see me home, was filled with fear when I approached him. To my surprise, I heard myself saying, "Welcome home, son!" and I extended my hand to him. Then I invited him to sit close to me in the living room for a personal talk. I heard myself expressing my love for him. I talked with him about the battle that every one of us has to fight each day within ourselves.

As I expressed my confidence in him, he broke into tears and began confessing his unworthiness, condemning himself beyond measure. Now it was my turn to put his transgression in proper perspective and to comfort him. A wonderful spirit came over us, and we ended up crying together, hugging each other in love and finally in joy. What might have been a disastrous confrontation between father and son became, with help from the power above, one of the most beautiful experiences of our relationship that we have ever had, an experience we have never forgotten. I testify that when we exercise the love of God's power as he has commanded us to do, our marriages and our families will be strengthened.

Elder James M. Paramore

LOVE ONE ANOTHER

A missionary in Italy recounted that one morning a poor little crippled boy in ragged clothes and badly worn shoes came to a busy street corner and went from person to person, begging for a few lira without success. A man observing the boy from a distance finally went over and picked up the lad, held him tightly and loved him, and then went forth and cared for him with his means without any judgment.

This sight would have touched any heart and helps us see the power of love that our Father in heaven would have us understand in our lives. Jesus, the beloved Son of God, re-emphasized this new dimension to bless the world when he said, "A new commandment I give unto you, That ye love one another." (John 13:34.)

As we step back and try to understand this love of God, we are astounded by its profound impact. At its center is the reality of a literal Father in heaven whose love for his children knows no bounds. He desires to share with his children, whom he created and sent to earth, all truth, wisdom, power, goodness, and love. He would have us reach up and know him as a Father, as one who forgives, as a helper, as friend, as lawgiver—as one anxious to grant to every person the full opportunity of his love and potential, and ultimately the blessing to one day become like him. This love from Father in heaven and its effects upon *one* of his children or the whole world is miraculous and contagious. He is constantly and everlastingly watching over us to lovingly and gently nudge us along.

He reaches down through his Son, through prayer, through his spirit and his prophets, and through his commandments to express his love and concern and provide his guidance and discipline to everyone who will listen. As the Psalmist said, "The earth is full of the goodness of the Lord." (Psalm 33:5.)

He loves us so much that he gave us his most sacred eternal truths: his commandments—eternal standards to live by. To help us understand their importance, he revealed and surrounded them in sacred and holy settings. Who does not remember how the Ten Commandments were given? Men have constantly changed these commandments, but we testify to the world that they have been restored on this earth through a prophet of God because they are essential, eternal truths, and, if they are altered by man, they lose their power. We testify to the world that these laws—commandments, standards—are one of the highest manifestations of the love God has for his children. Yes, they are commandments—absolutes—to plant the seeds of God's love, his ways, and his divinity in us. They are the fountainhead of all real security, and the inner soul recognizes this instinctively and rejoices.

This same loving God also "so loved the world, that he gave his only begotten Son" (John 3:16) to perform a myriad of blessings for all mankind, including the offering of his own life to atone for mankind. He lived his life to demonstrate that the love of our Father in heaven and his plan, his commandments, could in fact bring inner peace and lift mankind here and hereafter.

My assignments for the Church have taken me to many lands, and with all my heart I bear witness to the fact that when God's love is known and felt and his commandments are followed, the results are always the same. There is a newness of life, a spiritual awakening, that comes to us, its own witness that it is true. It is never forced or brought about by fear, but rather by a bond of love that develops between our Father in heaven and his children. It is no wonder that we are counseled to look to God and live. This love reaches deep into the inner soul, removes barriers, and causes an open spirit to emerge to be receptive to truth, goodness, and change. As it develops in us, we are turned outward toward others—gradually overcoming ourselves. When we humbly seek our Father in heaven through prayer and by learning and keeping his commandments, he transfers to us his love and many of his powers. Thousands bear witness that his words—"If ye keep my commandments, ye shall abide in my love" (John 15:10) —are true. We then, as the Savior said, begin to attach ourselves as branches to the "true vine" and receive the same strength and power and can expect the same fruit. (See John 15:1-6.)

Then the miracle really happens. Persons thus touched and changed by this love of God begin to look upon their neighbors with profound respect and awe for who they are, what their potential really is as children of an eternal Father.

I had a very special experience a few years ago on an assignment to Oregon. After a stake conference, I was asked to bless a little child. A couple were ushered into a room, and I learned that day what the love of God really is. They had adopted six or seven abandoned, physically handicapped children who would need their love and care the rest of their lives. I felt humble in their presence, and the love of God filled that room that day. They were no more strangers to God.

As we perceive this love, we begin to overlook the flaws that make up every mortal being and to esteem our brother as ourselves. (See D&C 38:24.) We lift and desire to help others whenever and wherever we can. Our spirits reach out to everyone, for now there is no enmity, no envy, no restricting philosophies, pride, or vanity—even language does not separate us; there is only an openness and oneness with the Spirit and the will of God. The scriptures are beautiful and clear: "There [will be] no contention in the land," "because the love of God is shed abroad in our hearts." (4 Nephi 1:15; Romans 5:5.)

Does this mean that those who embrace these things will be perfect? No, for they will forever be overcoming and growing. But it does mean that they will be striving toward perfection. The great prophet Moroni counseled us with a profound insight on this point when he said, "Condemn me not because of mine imperfection, neither my father, . . . but rather give thanks unto God that he hath made manifest unto you our imperfections, that ye may learn to be more wise than we have been." (Mormon 9:31.)

It is by achieving this gift, this love of God, that we are able to crowd out contention, discord, and judgments. It recognizes the power and goodness innate in mankind and how totally inconsistent it would be for those having these feelings—this love from God in their lives—to find themselves judging others and not sustaining their leaders, for these things are absolutely foreign to the love of God. Our Father in heaven said that "no one can assist in this work except he shall be humble and full of love." (D&C 12:8.)

As in the case of the man who picked up the little crippled boy, there are no reproachments or judgments—just love and help.

How is this love of God manifest today upon the earth and in his church and among its members?

By a Father in heaven who sent his beloved Son to help man to see his example and follow.

By a Father in heaven who has established his kingdom, his church, his love and commandments here upon this earth wherein all his blessings may be had and his love felt.

By a loving Father in heaven who has provided a prophet and apostles to receive his word and guide his children.

By families who are filled with this love and gratitude to God, reaching out every day to teach their children the peaceable things of God.

By fathers and mothers and children who, touched by the love of God, unashamedly take each other in their arms often and openly express their love and never give up on those within their circle who especially need their love.

By nearly thirty thousand missionaries who, at their own expense, go forth in love to the people everywhere on this earth and take these powers to all who will listen.

And by wonderful leaders and teachers who, though imperfect, reach out to our children and youth in countless ways to help them build bridges to God—his love and goodness.

Some time ago as I sat in a sacrament meeting in Germany, tears of gratitude filled my eyes and my heart was full. I saw eighty-two little children sing songs of love to their Heavenly Father. I was so grateful for the Church, which has been reestablished upon the earth, and that I too had one day been a Primary child, and my children also, and had learned those songs and the love they express. I've sung those songs many times since my youth and am grateful for the love and the message they bring. On this very same day, I met a new convert who was awaiting the arrival of her first child. She was very touched by the children, the Church, the Primary, and the love of our Heavenly Father that was there. She later excitedly said, "Oh, I can hardly wait to have my child so she can go to Primary."

This is only one of the many great programs and blessings that our Father in heaven has provided in his church, The Church of Jesus Christ of Latter-day Saints. Yes, there is a place of beauty—a refuge upon the earth—where the unchanging standards revealed by a loving Father in heaven are found. We invite all persons with all our love to come and partake of this spirit, this peace, this love of God that is in his kingdom upon the earth today.

Elder Loren C. Dunn

THE GOSPEL OF LOVE

A favorite hymn among Latter-day Saints today was also reported to be among the favorite hymns of the Prophet Joseph Smith and was sung in those fateful hours prior to his martyrdom. The words of the first verse go this way:

> *A poor wayfaring Man of grief*
> *Hath often crossed me on my way,*
> *Who sued so humbly for relief*
> *That I could never answer nay.*
> *I had not power to ask his name,*
> *Whereto he went, or whence he came;*
> *Yet there was something in his eye*
> *That won my love; I knew not why.*
> *(Hymns, 1985, no. 29.)*

The other verses of this hymn show that our love toward our fellowmen is indeed an expression of our love toward our God.

The greatest expression of love from our Father in heaven to the human family is probably the infinite atonement of the Savior. "God so loved the world," said John, "that he gave his only begotten Son, that whosoever believeth in him should not perish, but have everlasting life." (John 3:16.)

The most noble expression of love by man is "Love the Lord thy God with all thy heart, and with all thy soul, and with all thy mind. . . . And the second is like unto it, Thou shalt love thy neighbour as thyself." (Matthew 22:37, 39.)

To love our neighbor is a godlike trait and can take many forms.

On the day that no one in the neighborhood saw "Hanse," as she was called, concerned neighbors rang her doorbell, but to no avail. They were anxious for this gentle and gracious widow who found a place in their hearts. They looked on her as one of their own. Finally, a member of the bishopric forced open the door, and there, in the bedroom, was Marie Woodruff Hansen, as if she had fallen asleep, but never again to awaken in this life.

As the bishopric member paused to take in this sad but peaceful scene, he was startled to hear, from behind him, the words "I love you." Knowing that Marie lived alone, he turned, and there in the corner was a bird cage. A second time the bird said, "I love you." It was as if Marie herself had paused at the portals that mark the point between life and death to send back one final message before moving on to that new day.

Beyond her was a neighborhood of friends, both young and old. She knew them all. They were like family to her. Marie's baked goodies found their way into their homes, and they looked after her like a favorite aunt or a grandmother. Home teaching and visiting teaching were only the beginning as the whole neighborhood was caught up in this love affair. Children were welcomed into her home. They always knew there would be fresh-baked cookies. There was a warmth about that little home that was a reflection of Marie's whole life. Many prayers had been offered there: prayers of gratitude, prayers of thanksgiving.

The words Marie taught her pet bird were the words she lived by. Even in death they echoed in the ears of those she left behind. Ahead of her was a husband who had gone first, too many years ago. She had lived a full life and left one final message of goodbye in the words she knew best: "I love you."

Marie Hansen left a great legacy, probably greater than she realized. For did not the Savior say, "A new commandment I give unto you, That ye love one another; as I have loved you, that ye also love one another"? (John 13:34.)

There are those who wish to know us better, to understand us better as a religion, as a church. There are those who write about us and study us. But may I suggest that until they take into account this spirit of love, they will never really understand. At the heart of it all is a genuine love of God and of fellowman. Today, for instance, there are scores of Latter-day Saint missionaries in many countries throughout the world. They are easily identified by their dress and manner. They go on their missions for many reasons: duty, service, the testimony they have of their message. But after serving honorably for eighteen months or two years, virtually all of them develop a deep and profound love for the people they serve among. One missionary put it this way: "Although it was hard, I am thankful for all the experiences I've had here. They were right about the mission field; it's the best place to practice true Christianity, and it's the best time of your life." Another said: "I thank the Lord with all my heart for giving me the opportunity to serve him. I love this great land, and I love these people."

In Cali, Colombia, the mission president visited one of our church meetings. At the start of the meeting a seven-year-old boy came up on the stand and sat next to him. He was not on the program; he just wanted to be there. When the meeting was nearly over, the youth strode to the pulpit and bore his testimony. When he finished, he went back and sat next to the president. The two exchanged glances. The mission president smiled approval. The young boy smiled back. In those dark eyes was a message of love and security. Here was someone who knew he belonged.

Later it was learned that the boy had spent his earlier life as an orphan. A couple in the ward had taken him in and were raising him as their own. The whole ward was his home, and he was blossoming in this atmosphere of acceptance.

"Inasmuch as ye have done it unto one of the least of these my brethren, ye have done it unto me." (Matthew 25:40.)

A few years ago, President and Sister Spencer W. Kimball were touring missions overseas. A change in the airline schedule found them, along with a mission president and his wife, in a cold and drafty airport, late at night, with no place to go and nothing to do but wait for an early morning flight. Sister

Kimball had her coat, but the mission president's wife did not. President Kimball tried to give her his coat, but she would not take it. As they began to fall asleep on those hard benches, President Kimball got up and gently put his coat over the sleeping wife of the mission president.

This kind of selfless concern for others is how President Kimball lived his life. He literally spent his life in taking off his coat, so to speak, and putting it around the shoulders of those he judged to be in greater need: people of all colors and creeds; men, women, and children. It never made any difference to him. All were his brothers. All were his sisters.

"Charity suffereth long, and is kind, and envieth not, and is not puffed up, seeketh not her own, is not easily provoked, thinketh no evil, and rejoiceth not in iniquity but rejoiceth in the truth, beareth all things, believeth all things, hopeth all things, endureth all things. . . . [For] charity is the pure love of Christ, and it endureth forever." (Moroni 7:45, 47. See also 1 Corinthians 13.)

Some time ago Sister Dunn and I attended a stake conference in Marilia, Brazil. Marilia is a beautiful city of 100,000 in the southeast interior of the country. The Sunday session had just concluded. The theme was the atonement of Christ and how he is the Savior of the whole world. Some had traveled by bus for more than three hours to be at this meeting. As we were shaking hands, a young lady came up. She first stopped in front of the mission president and asked how to say "I love you" in English. She then stood in front of Sister Dunn and me and with a broad smile and great sincerity said "I love you." It seemed a little thing, but it touched our hearts. It was the effort of a humble follower of Christ to express herself. The message could have been said in any language and been understood.

The spirit of love reaches across language barriers. There is a purity about it that lifts the soul and causes us all to realize that we are the children of the same God.

There is a thread running through the examples of Marie Hansen; an orphan boy in Colombia; the young lady in Brazil; President Spencer W. Kimball. No one professes to be perfect, but there is a spirit in this work and among this people that makes them better than they would otherwise be. It is the spirit of love borne on the wings of the restored gospel of Jesus Christ. It comes from a God of love. It causes the Church to reach out to the lives of men and women everywhere.

The final verse of the hymn that I mentioned in the beginning goes like this:

> *Then in a moment to my view*
> *The stranger started from disguise;*
> *The tokens in his hands I knew;*
> *The Savior stood before mine eyes.*
> *He spake, and my poor name he named,*
> *"Of me thou hast not been ashamed;*
> *These deeds shall thy memorial be,*
> *Fear not, thou didst them unto me."*

We claim no corner on love of others. We know the world is filled with many good, decent people. We respect and admire them and the righteous things they stand for. We teach the gospel of Jesus Christ. It is a gospel of salvation and exaltation. It is a gospel of love—love of God and love of fellowmen.

Elder Marwin J. Ashton

WE SERVE THAT
WHICH WE LOVE

Just before six o'clock one morning, my wife and I boarded
a taxi in San Francisco during a short layover on a trip to Salt
Lake City from Australia. Our driver, who had been on duty
since three o'clock that morning, was anxious to talk with us,
his first passengers of the day. We learned that his parents, who
were born just outside Mexico City, moved to Chicago, where
he was born, and then to New Mexico. Twenty years earlier our
friend had come for a short visit to San Francisco and had never
left. During our trip to the airport, he related a few incidents
from which some great truths were reemphasized.

His parents, he told us, had remained in New Mexico, but
they liked to visit him and his brother whenever they could
afford it because they loved being with their children and
grandchildren. In New Mexico his mother's health was rather
poor, but whenever she was in San Francisco, she seemed to
feel much better. This discerning son had said to his brother, "I
know exactly what mother needs." Then he told us, "I found a
large truck, and my brother and I drove to New Mexico. We
loaded our parents and all their possessions into the truck, and
brought them to live near those who loved them most. Mother's

health improved noticeably." Then he added, "You know, love is very important if it is done right."

The second incident related by this humble but wise man is also significant. He said, "I teach all my children to work. I want them to have schooling, but they must learn to work to get it. I just finished helping my sixteen-year-old son get a part-time job at a bank. While he is going to school, he only works two hours a day, but he is learning to work. He knows I love him, because I do my part too. Because of the uncertainty of my driving hours, I can't always take him to work, but I'm always there to bring him home. He looks forward to our ride together, and so do I."

One other important point was made by this unusual taxi operator. He told us that some of his unmarried friends who are also taxi drivers are often out of money. They come to him to borrow, and he indicated that he is generally able to help them. When his companions ask how he is able to support his family on his salary when they can't even keep themselves, he said, "I don't waste money at the races or on liquor or tobacco. My wife fixes our meals at home, so we don't have to pay for expensive restaurant food." He smiled when he added, "We do our partying with our family." This man's objectives are family oriented, and he has learned the folly of serving momentary expensive habits.

A happy man, this driver. He has realized through experience important areas of love. He knows that nurturing love is healing; it is teaching. He knows that such love requires sacrifice, and that that which we love will be that to which we give our allegiance. He shared with us some basic principles of love in action that were potent. Frankly, we were enjoying his comments so much that we almost wished the airport terminal were another half hour away.

This taxi driver knew where to place his love. We, too, must choose carefully the areas in which we serve, because where we serve, there will be our love. During our lifetime, areas of love must be put in proper perspective.

In childhood we anxiously strive to ride a bicycle, to skate, to ski, to learn the laws of balance. Then our love of wheels and speed and balance becomes one of the joys of life. As we mature and serve and sacrifice for other interests, new loves develop. A farmer grows to love his land; a scholar, his books; a businessman, his company. We have all witnessed the love of parents for their children, the love of a bishop for members of his ward, the love of a young man for his new car, the love of a newly engaged woman for the ring received from someone very special.

Equally apparent in the world today is love many have for that which is evil. We jeopardize our future by loving and sacrificing for that which is not conducive to our health or our progress.

Many today are caught up in their love for worldly goods that they think will bring them fame, fortune, and popularity. They, too, reap the rewards of loving incorrectly, for that which they serve they will learn to love. What we learn to love can make or break our lives.

Love of money, drugs, and alcohol can turn men into thieves, murderers, and derelicts. First they love the effects of those evil things, then they sacrifice all—life, health, and liberty—for what they think are treasures. Love of the sensual, of drugs, and of lies grows as we serve in these areas made so appealing by Satan. Bonds of love become strong and intense in proportion to our continuing service. A man who learns to love a lie serves dishonesty all his life. In fact, a drug addict can usually be cured more quickly than can a liar.

One of the greatest accomplishments of Satan in these last days is his success in turning men's affection toward the destructive, the fleeting, the worldly. Rather than planning for that which is best for all, the world is becoming increasingly "me" centered. On every hand we hear many group leaders say, "We have a right," "We demand." Many young people believe that love has "rights" one can demand of a loved one. For example, a young man may say, "If you love me, you will let me . . . " He would take what he supposes are his rights rather than serving the higher standards of morality. Such a request does not bespeak love. Day-to-day acts of service, whether for good or evil, may not seem important, but they build cords of love that become so strong they can seldom be broken. Our responsibility is to place our areas of love in proper perspective. Meaningful love always works for eternal progress and not against it.

One who loves has and feels responsibility. The apostle Paul says that love "suffereth long, and is kind; . . . seeketh not her own, . . . thinketh no evil." (1 Corinthians 13:4-5.) If we look at love between two people who are preparing for temple marriage, we see the elements of sacrifice and of serving each other's best interest, not a short-sighted "me" interest. True love and happiness in courtship and marriage are based upon honesty, self-respect, sacrifice, consideration, courtesy, kindness, and placing "we" ahead of "me." Those who would have us forfeit virtue and chastity to prove our love in participating in sex out of wedlock are neither friends nor eternal-family oriented. To classify them as selfish and unwise is not too severe. Those who serve the flesh will never know the love and fruits of purity.

A convert to the Church shared this story: "I was in and out of enforced confinement most of my teen years. It wasn't so bad being there, because the food was pretty good, and we were treated all right. But it did get boring, so when anyone had any reading material, funny books, magazines, or anything, we would trade our food for a chance to borrow those items. One day I saw a fellow with a nice, thick book. I knew it would take a long time to read, so I offered him my pork chops, my potatoes, and all my main course food items for a week. He accepted my offer and loaned me the book. As I read it, I knew I was reading something very special and very true. The book for which I had sacrificed my food was titled the Book of Mormon. When I had a chance, I found the missionaries, changed my habits, and am now finding a new way of life. I love that book for which I traded my food."

Here was an unusual but worthwhile sacrifice with rewarding results. This convert indicated that the more time he spends with this book, the greater his love becomes for the truths he is finding between its covers.

Choose carefully what and whom you will serve or for what you will sacrifice, because that is where your love will be placed. It is important not only to love well, but also to love prudently. What we love takes our time. That to which we give time, we are apt to love. Our daily actions determine where our love will be.

Love for one's family is not the love of a martyr. Think back about the practical sermon of our taxi driver: "I teach my children to work, but I let them know I care. I do my part too." Our time, the listening ear, the understanding heart, and the unconditional love, even the opening of doors of opportunity at times, are some ways to serve those we love. But if we deprive family members of opportunity for their own actions, if we use them to further our own ambitions, then we do not serve them well or love them prudently. Wise love of family and people takes time.

If we give our children opportunities to work and contribute in the home, their love of family will increase. As they are encouraged to give time and sacrifice to develop their talents, whether they be academic or in music, drama, sports, leadership, or whatever, they will develop love for that which brings them success. Children will love those talents or possessions to which we encourage them to give time and effort.

As adults, if our top priorities are constantly directed toward the acquisition of more and better worldly goods, it will not take long to increase our love in those directions. The purchase of a larger house or a nicer car or a more expensive boat may cause us to sacrifice our resources and develop an unwise love for these symbols of success and pleasure. We learn to love that which we serve, and we serve that which we love.

How can we decrease our love for things not for our best good? We must examine our lives and see what services we are rendering and what sacrifices we are making, and then stop the expenditure of time and effort in these directions. If this can be managed, that love will wither and die. Our love should be channeled into sources that are eternally oriented. Our neighbors and families will respond to our love if we will but follow through with sustaining support and self-sharing. True love is as eternal as life itself. Some callings and assignments in the Church may seem insignificant and unimportant at the time, but with each willingly fulfilled assignment, love of the Lord will grow. We learn to love God as we serve and know him.

How can we help new converts to learn to love the gospel? By finding ways for them to serve and sacrifice. We must constantly emphasize the truth that we love that to which we give time, whether it be the gospel, God, or gold. Often we hear expressions of love for the scriptures, including Jesus' teachings. Those who study, practice, and apply the truths not only know them best, but are also fortified to use them for guidance all along life's paths. Those who most appreciate the opportunity to pay tithing are they who experience the joys and blessings that come through sacrifice, application, and obedience to the law of the tithe. Our appreciation and love of the gospel and its teachings will always be in proportion to our service and commitment to the gospel.

The greatest example of love available to all of us is, of course, found in the scriptures: "For God so loved the world, that he gave his only begotten Son." (John 3:16.) By the greatest of all acts of love and by this supreme sacrifice, God set the pattern. He demonstrated to us that his love is unconditional and is sufficient to encircle every person.

While Jesus was on earth, he taught us ways to use love correctly. We recall that when the scribes and Pharisees brought before him a woman taken in adultery, their purpose was not to show love for either the woman or Jesus, but to embarrass and trick him. They quoted the law of Moses, which said, "Such should be stoned," and asked of the Master, "What sayest thou?" The accusers walked away one by one when Jesus encouraged the one without sin to cast the first stone. We recall that Jesus asked of the woman, "Where are those thine accusers? hath no man condemned thee?" She answered, "No man, Lord." And Jesus said to her, "Neither do I condemn thee: go, and sin no more." (John 8:3-11.)

Jesus did not condone adultery—there is no doubt about his attitude toward moral conduct. He chose to teach with love, to show the scribes and Pharisees the need of serving the individual for her best good, and to show how destructive are trickery and embarrassment. He demonstrated that under all circumstances there is a proper way to show love. Perhaps our taxi driver has learned to apply the same Christian principle in his life when he wisely said, "You know, love is very important if it is done right." The Savior's conduct would entitle all of us to conclude that love is right when it is channeled to proper areas and given the right priority in our lives.

We live in a complex world where many forces are calling

out, "Love me." A sure way to set our guidelines for that which we choose to serve and learn to love is to follow the admonition of Joshua: "As for me and my house, we will serve the Lord." (Joshua 24:15.) Let us look to our own lives. We serve that which we love. If we sacrifice and give our love for that which our Father in heaven asks of us, our footsteps will be set upon the path of eternal life. May God help us to love the right, love the truth, and love areas of service that are rewarding and eternal.

Elder Jack H. Goaslind

REACH OUT TO OUR FATHER'S CHILDREN

As I read the account of the Savior's resurrection, I am impressed that the Savior's first words as a resurrected being provide the foundation for our relationships with others.

You will recall that early in the morning of the first day of the week, Mary had gone to the sepulchre where they had placed the Lord's body. Finding the stone that sealed the tomb removed, she ran and told Peter and John that the Lord's body had been taken. The two disciples hurried to the tomb to confirm this report. When they saw the empty tomb, they returned to their homes. But Mary Magdalene "stood without at the sepulchre weeping: and as she wept, she stooped down, and looked into the sepulchre." There she saw two angels in white. They asked her, "Why weepest thou?" She replied, "Because they have taken away my Lord, and I know not where they have laid him."

Having said this, Mary turned around and saw Jesus, but she did not recognize him. The Savior also asked why she was weeping. Mary said, thinking she was talking to the gardener, "Sir, if thou have borne him hence, tell me where thou hast laid him, and I will take him away." (John 20:11-15.) The Savior then called her by name, as he also could each of us, and she

49

immediately recognized him. Because of her great love for him and her witness that he lives, she extended her arms to embrace him. With love, concern, and assurance, he spoke these eternally significant words: "Touch me not; for I am not yet ascended to my Father: but go to my brethren, and say unto them, I ascend unto my Father, and your Father; and to my God, and your God." (John 20:17.)

"To my Father, and your Father; to my God, and your God." How important this message was then, and how vital it is for us today! The apostle Paul clearly taught the same doctrine when he said: "For in him we live, and move, and have our being; as certain also of your own poets have said, For we are also his offspring. Forasmuch then as we are the offspring of God, we ought not to think that the Godhead is like unto gold, or silver, or stone, graven by art and man's device." (Acts 17:28-29.)

Through prayer, study, and living the gospel, I have come to appreciate the fact that we are all our Father's children, part of one large family. We are sons and daughters of God. Our Heavenly Father is in a very real sense the actual Father of our spirits, which gives literal significance to the phrase "Our Heavenly Father." It follows that we are all brothers and sisters regardless of race, creed, or nationality. There is a spark of divinity in each of us.

How should this truth affect our relationships with others? If all of God's children truly realized and felt the impact of this great truth, there would be far more understanding, compassion, and love shown to one another. Wars, crime, and all forms of cruelty would cease. I am convinced that true brotherly love is essential to our happiness and to world peace. We must love one another and unselfishly share our gifts, talents, and resources.

William Shakespeare once said, "They do not love that do not show their love." *(The Two Gentlemen of Verona,* act 1, sc. 2, line 31.) We need to show our love, beginning in the home and then widening our circle of love to encompass our ward members, our less active and nonmember neighbors, and also those who have passed beyond the veil.

To leaders in the Church, to every member, may I ask you to reach out as never before and extend the hand of fellowship to our brothers and sisters who need the light of the gospel. I am persuaded that much of our love is confined to mere lip service and dreams of good deeds accomplished, but true love must be expressed in unselfish acts of kindness that bring others closer to our Heavenly Father.

How often I think of the great example of Peter and John as they approached the temple at the hour of prayer. A certain man, lame from his birth, was laid at the gate called Beautiful to ask alms of those who entered. When he saw Peter and John approaching, he extended his hand for their contribution. Peter said to him, "Look on us." He immediately gave heed, expecting to receive something of them. Instead, Peter said, "Silver and gold have I none; but such as I have give I thee: In the name of Jesus Christ of Nazareth rise up and walk." I believe that this is as far as we have gone, in most cases, in helping our fellowmen in today's world. However, Peter did not stop with mere words. The scripture records that he then "took him by the right hand, and lifted him up," and immediately the man's feet and ankles received strength and he stood, walked, leaped, and entered the temple praising God. (See Acts 3:1-9.)

It isn't silver and gold that the world needs today, but the extended hand and the lifting influence of the Spirit of the Lord.

A good friend shared a story about how she learned the deeper meaning of love. Her parents have always been active in the Church, trying their best to live the commandments. They were shocked and disappointed, however, when their daughter became engaged to a nonmember.

The next day the mother was telling a good friend about her feelings. She knew her daughter's fiance was a fine young man, but she felt angry, hurt, betrayed, and numb and did not want to give her daughter a wedding or even see her. She said that the Lord must have guided her to talk to her friend, because she received this reply: "What kind of a mother are you that you only love her when she does what you want her to do? That is selfish, self-centered, qualified love. It's easy to love our children when they are good; but when they make mistakes, they need our love even more. We should love and care for them no matter what they do. It doesn't mean we condone or approve of the errors, but we help, not condemn; love, not hate; forgive, not judge. We build them up rather than tear them down; we lead them, not desert them. We love when they are the most unlovable, and if you can't or won't do that, you are a poor mother."

With tears streaming down her face, the mother asked her friend how she could ever thank her. The friend answered, "Do it for someone else when the need arises. Someone did it for me, and I will be eternally grateful."

This story concerns a mother's love for her daughter. But this is only the beginning. We must show such genuine love for all our Father's children. When we learn to do this, we will be truly godlike. As John wrote, "Beloved, let us love one another: for love is of God; and every one that loveth is born of God and knoweth God. He that loveth not knoweth not God; for God is love." (1 John 4:7-8.)

Jesus Christ, our perfect exemplar, consistently demonstrated his love through acts of compassion, and he understood the most appropriate ways to express love. At Jacob's well, he took the time to teach a woman of Samaria some glorious eternal truths. She accepted his testimony that he was the Messiah, and she returned to the city to testify, "Is not this the Christ?" (John 4:29.)

He gave of himself to the outcasts of society. A despised leper worshiped the Lord and said, "Lord, if thou wilt, thou canst make me clean." The scripture records that "Jesus put forth his hand, and touched him, saying, I will; be thou clean. And immediately his leprosy was cleansed." (Matthew 8:2-3.)

In one of his most dramatic miracles, Jesus still paid attention to individuals. As he prepared to raise Lazarus from the dead, he saw Mary weeping, and, the record states, "he groaned in the spirit, and was troubled." And then, "Jesus wept." (John 11:33-35.) He used this occasion to express a divine testimony of his mission: "I am the resurrection, and the life: he that believeth in me, though he were dead, yet shall he live." (John 11:25.)

In his visit to the Nephites, the Savior gave this important admonition: "Therefore, what manner of men ought ye to be? Verily I say unto you, even as I am." (3 Nephi 27:27.)

It is my witness that we can be even as he is. We can

demonstrate our love in ways that have eternal benefits both for ourselves and for those we serve. Let us accept the challenge issued by President Spencer W. Kimball: "It seems clear to me—indeed, this impression weighs upon me—that the Church is at a point in its growth and maturity when we are at last ready to move forward in a major way.... But the basic decisions needed for us to move forward, as a people, must be made by the individual members of the Church. The major strides which must be made by the Church will follow upon the major strides to be made by us as individuals. We have paused on some plateaus long enough. Let us resume our journey forward and upward. Let us quietly put an end to our reluctance to reach out to others—whether in our own families, wards, or neighborhoods." (*Conference Report,* April 1979, p. 114.)

Let us decide today that we will reach out in love to our families, our less active or nonmember neighbors, our departed kindred, or anyone who has need of love. I testify that great blessings will come to us as individuals, as a church, and as a brotherhood of mankind when we learn to live outside ourselves in love.

Elder J. Richard Clarke

LOVE EXTENDS BEYOND CONVENIENCE

Salvation comes to us on an individual basis—each must climb the ladder independently to ascend to the level of the Master. If we are to achieve perfection, we must emulate his works as well as his words. The apostle Peter instructed those who would be disciples of Christ to be "partakers of the divine nature." (2 Peter 1:4-7.) He told them, "For even hereunto were ye called: . . . that ye should follow his steps." (1 Peter 2:21.)

In 1897 Dr. Charles Sheldon, a young minister in Topeka, Kansas, wrote a book that he titled *In His Steps*. It was a novel based upon an experiment he tried. He disguised himself as an unemployed printer and tramped the streets of Topeka. He was shocked at his treatment by this so-called Christian community. In his novel, a Christian minister presents his congregation with this interesting challenge: "I want volunteers . . . who will pledge themselves, earnestly and honestly for an entire year, not to do anything without first asking the question, 'What would Jesus do?' . . . Our aim will be to act just as He would if He [were] in our places, regardless of immediate results. In other words, we propose to follow Jesus' steps as closely and as literally as we believe He taught His disciples to do." (Charles M. Sheldon, *In His Steps,* New York: Grosset & Dunlap, 1935, pp. 15-16.)

The book describes the fascinating experience of those who accepted the challenge. I have been intrigued by the experiment and wonder, if it were conducted today among the Latter-day Saints, how we would measure up. As latter-day Christians, we know that the "royal law" (James 2:8) of love in action is to "succor the weak, lift up the hands which hang down, and strengthen the feeble knees." (D&C 81:5.) Do we catch the significance of this thought? We demonstrate the depth of our love for the Savior when we care enough to seek out the suffering among us and attend to their needs.

The philosopher William George Jordan has identified "four great hungers of life—body-hunger, mind-hunger, heart-hunger, and soul-hunger. They are all real; all need recognition, all need feeding." He explained:

1. Body-hunger is our most conscious biological need. It is difficult to be spiritually strong when temporally deficient.

2. Mind-hunger is a craving for intellectual food, for education, and for personal development.

3. Heart-hunger is to be lonely, to have low self-esteem, to feel misunderstood, to crave companionship, sympathy, and appreciation. However, we find that as we seek to satisfy the heart-hunger of our neighbor, we reduce our own.

4. Soul-hunger is the burning desire to know eternal truth. It is the yearning of the spirit to commune with God. (*The Crown of Individuality,* 1909, pp. 63-75.)

The restored gospel of Jesus Christ provides the solution to all the hungers of life. Jesus said: "I am the bread of life: he that cometh to me shall never hunger; and he that believeth on me shall never thirst." (John 6:35.) We would all like to have the Savior's capacity to assuage the hungers of the world; but let us not forget that there are many simple ways by which we can walk in his steps. Let us remember that in giving of ourselves, it is less a question of giving a lot than of giving at the right moment.

How many times have we observed a benevolent act performed by someone and asked ourselves, "Why didn't I think of that?" Those who do the deeds we would have liked to do seem to have mastered the art of awareness. They have formed the habit of being sensitive to the needs of others before they think of themselves. How swiftly opportunity slips away and we are left with another unfulfilled good intention. If only our acts of kindness could equal the righteous desires of our hearts.

When I think of performing deeds of kindness, I immediately think of bishops and Relief Society presidents. Relatively few people know of the many hours they selflessly spend in serving members of their wards. They truly translate principles into deeds. To illustrate, I quote this heartwarming pioneer account:

"Many years ago in a small town in the southern part of the state of Utah, my great-grandmother was called to be the president of the Relief Society. During this period of our Church's history there existed a very bitter and antagonistic spirit between the Mormons and the Gentiles.

"In my great-grandmother's ward one of the young sisters married a gentile boy. This of course did not please either the Mormons or the Gentiles very much. In the course of time this young couple gave birth to a child. Unfortunately the mother became so ill in the process of childbirth that she was unable to care for her baby. Upon learning of this woman's condition, great-grandmother immediately went to the homes of the sisters in the ward and asked them if they would take a turn going into the home of this young couple to care for the baby. One by one these women refused and so the responsibility fell completely upon her.

"She would arise early in the morning, walk what was a considerable distance to the home of this young couple where she would bathe and feed the baby, gather all that needed to be laundered and take it with her to her home.... One morning she felt too weak and sick to go.... However, as she lay in bed she realized that if she didn't go the child would not be provided for. [With the help of the Lord,] she mustered all her strength and went. [When she returned home, exhausted, she] collapsed into a large chair and immediately fell into a deep sleep. She said that as she slept she felt as if she were consumed by a fire that would melt the very marrow of her bones. She ... dreamed that she was bathing the Christ child and glorying in what a great privilege it would have been to have bathed the Son of God. Then the voice of the Lord spoke to her saying,

'Inasmuch as ye have done it unto the least of these, ye have done it unto me.'" (*My Errand from the Lord,* A Personal Study Guide for Melchizedek Priesthood Quorums 1976-77, pp. 154-55.)

Perhaps the most heroic acts are done quietly and with no recognition except from a loving Heavenly Father who rewards us with that sweet peace which passeth understanding (see Philippians 4:7) and by his Spirit whispers, "Well done, [my] good and faithful servant." (Matthew 25:21.)

I was touched by an experience that was recently related to me. A dear sister had been incapacitated for the past eight years—she could not walk or talk and was confined to bed. About six years ago, she and her husband were assigned a faithful home teacher. He asked if his wife could come over to their house every Sunday morning and stay with the invalid woman while her husband attended priesthood meeting. For six years, every Sunday this home teacher would bring his wife over to stay with the invalid sister while her husband went to his meeting. And every Sunday the home teacher's wife would bring with her some baked goods or something special that she had made for this older couple. Finally, this sister who had been ill passed away. When her daughter tried to express her deep love and appreciation to this loving home teacher and his wife for what they had done over the years, the wife said, "Oh, don't thank us. It was our *privilege* to visit with your sweet mother. What am I going to do now? The hour and a half on Sunday morning will now be, for me, the loneliest hour and a half in the week."

I am impressed that in the last moments of the Savior's life, he had an abiding concern for his mother and for her welfare, thus again setting the example for us. Walking in his steps are the devoted sons and daughters who honor aging parents who are no longer able to help themselves.

If we are to walk in the steps of the Savior, we cannot do it without personal sacrifice and sincere involvement. It is rarely convenient, but love extends beyond convenience for those who have conditioned themselves to look for opportunities to serve. I believe that the Savior was equipped to accomplish his mission not only through his parentage, but because of his thirty years of preparation in developing an awareness of and a sensitivity to the needs of his fellowmen.

In Alma, we read: "And he shall go forth, suffering pains and afflictions and temptations of every kind; . . . that the word might be fulfilled which saith he will take upon him the pains and the sicknesses of his people. . . . And he will take upon him their infirmities, that his bowels may be filled with mercy, according to the flesh, that he may know according to the flesh how to succor his people." (Alma 7:11-12.)

After a recent stake conference meeting where I had discussed the role of the family in the Church, I was approached by a sweet woman who said, "I'm a widow and I really appreciated everything you said today. I have a lovely family, but I have many problems and I do need help. My priesthood leaders have families of their own and they have lots of problems and I don't want to bother them and add to their problems. So what should I do?"

I asked her, "Do you have a good home teacher who really cares about you?"

She said, "Yes, I have a home teacher and he comes by every month or so; but he isn't very involved with our family."

Then I asked, "Well, do you have a visiting teacher who visits you and understands you?"

She said, "Yes, the Relief Society sometimes comes."

At this point I was praying for a right answer when a lovely sister, who was standing nearby and heard our conversation, said, "Excuse me, but I was a widow; and even though I have just remarried, I know how you feel and I understand your problems. Please let me drop by. I'd like to visit with you."

Dr. Tom Dooley offers some interesting insights regarding those who have known difficulties and can now share the burden of another: "One of Dr. [Albert] Schweitzer's most important concepts is that of the Fellowship of Those Who Bear the Mark of Pain. . . . Who are its members? Those who have learned by experience what physical pain and bodily anguish mean. These people, all over the world, are united by a secret bond. He who has been delivered from pain must not think he is now . . . at liberty to continue his life and forget his sickness. He is a man whose eyes are opened. He now has a duty to help others in their battles with pain and anguish. He must help to bring to others the deliverance which he himself knows. Under this Fellowship come not only whose who were formerly sick, but those who are related to sufferers, and whom does this not include?" (Thomas Dooley, "A Worldwide Fellowship," in *Words of Wisdom,* ed. Thomas C. Jones, Chicago: J. B. Ferguson, 1966, p. 150.)

Again I refer to Dr. Sheldon's book: "It is the personal element that Christian discipleship needs to emphasize. 'The gift without the giver is bare.' The Christianity that attempts to suffer by proxy [*alone*] is not the Christianity of Christ. Each individual Christian . . . needs to follow *in His Steps* along the path of personal sacrifice to Him. There is not a different path to-day from that of Jesus' own times. It is the same path." (*In His Steps,* p. 239; italics added.)

I bear my testimony that a special spirit of the Savior accompanies service. I know that he loves this work and the thousands of Saints who are engaged in it. And as he counseled his covenant people in the Book of Mormon, so he entreats us today: "Verily, verily, I say unto you, this is my gospel; and ye know the things that ye must do in my church; for the works which ye have seen me do that shall ye also do. . . . Therefore, if ye do these things blessed are ye, for ye shall be lifted up at the last day. . . . Therefore, what manner of men ought ye to be? Verily I say unto you, even as I am." (3 Nephi 27:21-22, 27.)

May we walk in his steps and become even as he is.

Elder H. Burke Peterson

THE DAILY PORTION OF LOVE

Some years ago in our ward fast and testimony meeting, a young father proudly gave a name and a blessing to his first child. Afterwards he stood to bear his testimony. He expressed thanks for this, his first son. He then said, in a rather perplexed way, that since the little fellow didn't seem to understand anything they said, he wished he knew just how to communicate with him. "All we can do," said he, "is hold him, cuddle him, gently squeeze him, kiss him, and whisper thoughts of love in his ear."

After the meeting I went up to the new father and said that in his testimony he had given us a success pattern for raising healthy children. I hoped he would never forget it; even as his children grew to maturity, I hoped he would continue the practice.

Among the tragedies we see around us every day are the countless children and adults who are literally starving because they are not being fed a daily portion of love. We have in our midst thousands who would give anything to hear the words and feel the warmth of this expression. We have all seen the lonely and discouraged who have never been told.

A few years ago I was assigned to tour a mission in a distant land. Before my first meeting with the missionaries, I asked the mission president if there were any particular problems I needed to attend to. He told me of one missionary who had made his mind up to go home early—he was very unhappy. "Could I help him?" I asked. The president wasn't sure.

As I was shaking hands with the missionaries before the meeting, it wasn't hard to tell which one wanted to leave. I told the president that if he didn't mind, I'd like to speak to the young man after the meeting. As I watched him during the meeting, about all I could think of was the big piece of gum he had in his mouth. After the meeting this tall young missionary came up to the stand. "Could we visit?" I asked. His response was an inference that he couldn't care less. We went to the side of the chapel. As we sat together, I gave him my very best speech on why missionaries should not go home early. He kept looking out the window, paying absolutely no attention to me.

Off and on we were in meetings together for two days. One time he even sat on the front row and read the newspaper as I talked. I was baffled and unnerved by him. By now it appeared to me that he should go home—and soon! I'd been praying for a way to reach him for two days, but to no avail.

After our meeting the last night, I stopped to visit with some folks in the front of the chapel. Out of the corner of my eye I saw the elder. At that very moment I had a feeling about him enter my heart that I had not yet experienced. I excused myself, went over to him, took his hand, looked him in the eye, and said, "Elder, I'm glad I've become acquainted with you. I want you to know that I love you."

Nothing more was said, and we separated. Then, as I started out the chapel door for our car, there he stood again. I took his hand again, put my arm around him, looked up in his eyes, and said, "What I said to you before, I really mean. I love you. Please keep in touch with me." Spirit communicates to spirit. It was then that his eyes filled with tears and this boy said simply, "Brother Peterson, in all my life I can never remember being told 'I love you.'"

Now I knew why he was confused, disturbed, insecure, and wanted to leave the mission field.

In speaking of a son or daughter, some will say, "He ought

to know I love him. Haven't I done everything for him? I buy him clothes, give him a warm home, an education, and so on." Make no false assumptions: unless the child feels that the need has been filled, the parent's responsibility has not been accomplished. We must make an even clearer effort to communicate real love to a questioning child. The giving of love from a parent to a son or daughter must not be dependent on his or her performance. Ofttimes those we think deserve our love the least need it the most.

Remember this scriptural admonition to parents: "And ye will not suffer your children that they go hungry, or naked; neither will ye suffer that they transgress the laws of God, and fight and quarrel one with another, and serve the devil, who is the master of sin, or who is the evil spirit which hath been spoken of by our fathers, he being an enemy to all righteousness. But ye will teach them to walk in the ways of truth and soberness; ye will teach them to love one another, and to serve one another." (Mosiah 4:14-15.)

May I suggest that parents' teachings will be listened to more intently and be heeded more closely if they are preceded by and woven together with that golden fiber of love. If our words are to be remembered, they must be accompanied and followed by considerate, thoughtful actions that cannot be forgotten.

Many are waiting for the other person to take the first step, to make the first overture. If you are a parent or a child, a husband or wife who has been waiting for another person to give some expression first, please heed this.

One of the most effective secrets for happiness is contained in the fourth chapter of 1 John, verse 19. It is only eight words long: "We love him, because he first loved us." This will cause a change to happen because it is right. "He first loved us." Your children will love you; your brothers and sisters will love you; your eternal companion will love you—because you first loved them. Now I don't mean it will all happen in a day, a week, or a year. But it will happen if you do not give up.

If you haven't been in the habit of expressing your love regularly, start out easily—maybe only as much as an eyedropper or two at first. At the beginning of this new approach, even a glassful could cause a drowning. Build up the dosage as tolerance to accept it grows. Whatever you give, be sincere and honest in your expression.

Impossible mountains are climbed by those who have the self-confidence that comes from truly being loved. Prisons and other institutions, even some of our own homes, are filled with those who have been starved for affection. In a world and society where Satan is launching his most vicious attacks ever on the children of men, we have no greater weapon than pure, unselfish, Christlike love.

Now I know that for some, this may not be an easy thing to start. Regardless of whether it is easy or hard for you, the Master gave the commandment to all—not to a few in one land or a handful in another, not just to a family here or there, but to all his children, everywhere. Express love now! Show it now, that we might enjoy the eternities together as families.

He told us: "A new commandment I give unto you, That ye love one another; as I have loved you, that ye also love one another. By this shall all men know that ye are my disciples, if ye have love one to another." (John 13:34-35.) We can all be his disciples.

Some time ago President Kimball passed me as we were rushing to a meeting. He stopped, took my hand, looked me in the eye, put away all of his other cares, and said simply, "I'm sorry we're sometimes so busy. I guess I haven't told you lately how much I love you and appreciate you." I felt his spirit; I believed him; my spirit soared to a new height.

If our love comes from the heart, it will work. It will bring peace and happiness to a troubled soul. Please try again . . . and again . . . and again. I know that he who set this pattern lives. I know that Jesus is the Christ. Of this I testify.

Elder Yoshihiko Kikuchi

THE MESSAGE OF LOVE

I am so grateful to the many missionaries who have come to my homeland of Japan. When I see their wonderful works, my heart turns to their parents who sent them and to those who are giving great sacrifices now that their sons and daughters may go on missions. I met a mother who was driving a taxi in Salt Lake City as a part-time job so she could send her son on his mission. She spoke very proudly of her son, who was on his mission serving his Father in heaven.

May I share with you a beautiful missionary experience I encountered recently? I saw a miracle performed by a missionary who so dearly loved an investigator. I met this gentleman at a special fireside. He said, "I appreciate very much the young Mormon missionary who taught me the most important thing in life and gave me happiness. Sometime I would like to extend my sincere appreciation to the parents who taught him to so live the gospel." With tears in his eyes, and as he was holding my hands, he said, "Oh, Elder Kikuchi, I thank our Heavenly Father for this glorious gospel," and then he related the following story:

"One day eight years ago, on my way home from work, I was hit by a hit-and-run driver. For eleven days I was unconscious, and for two years I was in a hospital. When I was finally released from the hospital, my wife had left me and had taken the children with her. We had had a fine family life before the accident, but my life became a total wreck. I was lonesome and depressed, for I had lost my most precious possession—my family. I attempted suicide many times. My only living came from welfare. I was emotionally and physically exhausted; I had become a living vegetable. I couldn't walk, so I would transport myself by rolling over on the floor and crawling on all fours.

"One evening I went to the hospital to see my doctor for the final results of a series of operations. He told me there was no hope for recovery. Though I had expected him to say so, it was still very shocking for me. All was lost. As I approached a railway bridge on my return from the doctor's, I wept to see my own face in the wet reflection on the pavement. It was a pitiful sight."

Just when this man was about to jump in front of the oncoming train, he met one of our missionaries. Cottage meetings began immediately. In them, Mr. Sugiyama learned that the gospel is true, that Jesus Christ is our Savior, that Joseph Smith was a prophet of God, and that the true church of God has been restored in this last dispensation.

As usual, missionaries invited him to church; however, because he couldn't walk, he said he wouldn't be able to come. But on the morning of the Sabbath, he awoke early and bravely headed for the church. Though it was close, it took him nearly three hours to traverse the distance between his home and the closest station to the Yokohama chapel. The Yokohama chapel is situated high upon a hill. It took him almost an hour to go from the station to the church, although ordinarily it would take a person only five minutes. He would cling to the wall, then fall down, only to struggle again to his feet. He finally reached the chapel, where the sacrament was in progress. The missionaries had never expected him to come to church. But Brother Sugiyama felt the pure love of God from the missionaries and members and felt himself drawn to it. Shortly afterward, he followed the Lord's commandment by being baptized.

The morning following his baptism, Brother Sugiyama woke up bright and early. He stretched his legs out in preparation to roll over as usual. But this time, something was different. He felt strength in his legs, and his whole body surged with power. He sat up and gradually, eventually, stood on his feet.

He hadn't stood for years without other supports. He walked away that morning! He found that his body had been made whole.

Said the Savior to a similar one who had been healed by faith, "Thy faith hath made thee whole; go in peace." (Mark 5:34.) Brother Sugiyama said, "Love hath made me whole, and I will go in peace in the Lord's way." Miracles are not the only evidences of the true Church of God, but we can learn much from the miracle performed by the Lord through a great young Mormon missionary who loved his investigator so much.

Love precedes the miracle. Love is a process; it is not a program. The love of Christ can overcome any of the worries of our lives and heal any human affliction. To all my friends wherever they may be, let us come unto Jesus and "be born of water and of the Spirit." (John 3:5.) For as the Lord said, "Whosoever believeth on my words, them will I visit with the manifestation of my Spirit; and they shall be born of me, even of water and of the Spirit." (D&C 5:16.)

Oh, how I appreciate my own missionaries who taught me the most glorious message that we can hear! Elder Law and Elder Porter, I thank you. Oh, how many lives have been touched by missionaries like them! May we continue to send great missionaries from every nation as our prophet has asked us to do. And may we members of this true church have enough courage to stand before the world to share this great message of the everlasting gospel, the restored gospel of Jesus Christ, with "every nation, kindred, tongue, and people." (D&C 77:8.) We must be the light of the world. Someone is waiting there for us.

Elder Theodore M. Burton

THE NEED FOR LOVE

The basic need in the world today is for people to be taught true principles of love. I speak of love as meaning a lack of personal selfishness. True love is the exact opposite of the present philosophy of selfishness that seems to permeate the world. Selfish interests color people's dealings with each other and even color person-to-person contact within the family.

True love is based on personal unselfishness, but our modern world does not seem to understand this. People today seem to have lost their capacity to love. Jesus warned us that one of the principal characteristics of the last days would be that love among the people would gradually die. He said, "Because iniquity shall abound, the love of many shall wax cold." (Joseph Smith–Matthew 1:10. See also Matthew 24:12.) My thesis is that the iniquity of which he spoke is based on personal selfishness. That is the reason why love among the people is dying.

Jesus warned that iniquities in the last days would become so great "that, if possible, they shall deceive the very elect, who are the elect according to the covenant." (Joseph Smith–Matthew 1:22. See also Matthew 24:24.) I understand this to mean that eventually even the most faithful of the Lord's covenant Saints will become contaminated and threatened by modern-day philosophies. I believe that unless these days are shortened, none of us could long remain unaffected by such trends.

It may well be that the present attitude of personal selfishness is the cause of most of the unhappiness with life among the people of the world. This attitude shows up even in our daily occupations. For instance, when a man is offered a job, he seldom asks what opportunities the job offers to be of service to others. His first question is "What is there in this job for me?" The salary offered is too low. Having to move to or live in a given city is not convenient. He does not want to travel. He does not want to be confined to a desk, or he does not want to work such long hours. Before he even begins to work he asks, "What retirement benefits will I receive?" He is not interested in challenges, but only in security.

May I first speak to young people about personal selfishness in courtship? Actually, what is the main purpose for dating? Isn't it to get to know another person well enough to know what kind of a partner that person would be? Isn't it to learn to know that other person's character, interests, talents, and abilities? Or is dating merely an opportunity to satisfy one's passions? Each person will have to answer that question for himself or herself. However, a sure guide would be to follow the words of the Savior: "Again I say unto you, let every man esteem his brother as himself." (D&C 38:25.)

The necessity for practicing unselfish love in courtship becomes imperative in marriage. Persons interested only in romance soon find the realities of marriage too much to cope with. Yet in magazines and books emphasis is placed on romance and material pleasures. This is almost the exclusive appeal of advertising. It is demonstrated over and over again in moving pictures and on television. It is the exclusive appeal of pornographic literature. People become conditioned by this exposure and grow up expecting only personal gratification in marriage. Personal selfishness is the main reason for the present high divorce rate throughout the world.

The desire for personal gratification results in disharmony in marriage. Couples interested only in themselves don't communicate. Lack of communication then becomes a major stumbling block in developing true love. Lack of communication coupled with the postponement of children is based on selfishness, as is the greater evil of abortion. We shudder as we read in

Leviticus of the sacrifices of idol worshipers of that time who fed their children into the fiery maw of the iron god Molech. Is personal selfishness that results in abortion any less repulsive to God, as modern people through abortion offer the sacrifice of their children to their idol of selfish materialism?

Why bother to marry when children are neither wanted nor expected? Why burden oneself with marriage if couples expect to change partners when they tire of one another? What is the need for virtue when one's goal is only self-satisfaction? If ever there was a need for the restoration of truth in a world where man is only interested in his own pleasure and self-gratification, it is now!

As I see how many people quarrel and antagonize one another, I understand better why Jesus continually emphasized the need for love. The gospel of Jesus Christ is a gospel of love. A life of love is not an easy life to live, especially when one lives in a world where strife with neighbors and strife within one's own family is so common. People have been hurt so often in the past that they are constantly on guard against one another. They have drawn a defensive circle around themselves so tightly it is difficult to penetrate. Yet they need to be taught love.

Strife in families leads to wife abuse and child abuse. This, too, comes through personal selfishness. It is so common in the world that we even find it creeping into the Church. As the Church grows rapidly, we must teach love with increasing effectiveness. This is why our leaders continually caution home teachers to care for their families and "watch over the church always, and be with and strengthen them; and see that there is no iniquity in the church, neither hardness with each other, neither lying, backbiting, nor evil speaking." (D&C 20:53-54.)

Jesus, out of pure unselfish love, gave his life for our sake. Had he been as selfish as people are nowadays, there would have been no atonement. We would have been cut off from the presence of God forever and left to be carnal, sensual, and devilish. But Jesus was not selfish. He prepared a way whereby every individual may find personal happiness and great joy in life. That joy, however, must come in the Lord's way—through unselfish love.

I understand now why Jesus always spoke out so strongly

against disputations and contention. Contention is of the devil and not of God. I see the need for modern prophets to be in communication with God. I see their strivings to lead God's children toward truth and righteousness. Their message may be unpopular, but it is needed, for it is the only way to happiness. We are living in the last days. It is a day when love is waxing cold. People who will not listen to these warnings are preparing themselves for destruction. Jesus Christ will soon come in power and glory. When he comes, the only ones who will be spared are those who have learned to love God and one another with all their heart, might, mind, and strength.

Elder Rex D. Pinegar

THE GIFT OF LOVE

Recently a friend of mine was returning to Salt Lake City on a plane from Dallas, Texas. His mind was focused upon an important event that was soon to occur in his family. His only son would be leaving home in just a few days to serve as a missionary in a far-distant land. His great love for his son caused him to reflect, "If my son is going so far away to teach about our church, this had better be the best church!" Then he took out a notepad and pen and began to list the characteristics or qualities one would look for in the best church.

"There should be a program to build and strengthen youth," he wrote, "an athletic program, a wholesome activity program, a program for teaching and training children, a program for developing the skills and talents of women, a program to provide for the needy, for the ill, for the lonely, for victims of catastrophes and disasters, a program to provide opportunities for work and service, a program to assist families and individuals in spiritual development and progress."

His list became long and impressive, and he satisfied himself that his church, The Church of Jesus Christ of Latter-day Saints, offered a program to meet the need of every individual. Truly, he decided, it is the best church his son could represent.

My friend felt so good about his list of attractive qualities of the best church that he decided to show it to the gentleman seated next to him on the plane. The man, an executive with a financial firm, responded with interest and respect. Together they reviewed the list. Then the businessman asked my friend, "Would you like to know what I would look for in a church? There is just one criterion: the members of that church would best exemplify the teaching of the Savior: 'Love thy neighbour as thyself.'"

My friend said he learned an important lesson from that experience. He had taught this fine man about the programs of the Church without acknowledging that the purpose of these programs is to help members learn how to love God and their fellowmen. It is love for the Lord and for our neighbors—for all persons everywhere—that is the motivating force that prompts my friend's son, and twenty-seven thousand like him, to leave home, friends, family, security, and comfort to go among unknown neighbors throughout the world with the message of the gospel of Jesus Christ. It is because we love the Lord and our neighbor that we are willing to go to any length, sacrifice at any price, to share the message that has brought joy and happiness into our own lives. Latter-day Saints declare that God lives, that he loves all persons, and that he will lead to everlasting joy and happiness all who will repent and follow him.

We believe that the people of the world are yearning for a message such as this to believe in. A national survey conducted by a leading publishing company revealed that the people of the world are in desperate need of a religion that will "regenerate their underlying faith in Christian living, . . . that will help them find the strength within themselves which their forefathers had, . . . a religion that will bring back strong family relationships, . . . and a religion that reflects the pioneering strengths which built this great country." This survey discovered that the basic concepts of The Church of Jesus Christ of Latter-day Saints parallel the religious needs that people are seeking. The New York-based publishing company stated: "In a time of confusion, they [Mormons] give very clear and definite answers. . . . Their growth prospects for the immediate future seem very good . . . in that great world that is awaiting conversion." (Unpublished report, Littlepage Limited Advertising Co., Aug. 15, 1978.)

My daughter Kristen expressed a concern to me that I believe is felt by many who are seeking to find a better, more righteous way of life. She said, "Dad, I've been challenged to live just one day as Jesus would live, but I've tried for a week now and I just can't do it. Every day I think this will be that day. Then I make a mistake, and I have to wait for another day before I can try again."

I am often asked to counsel with people who experience somewhat that same dilemma. They want to correct and change their lives. They feel, however, that they have made so many mistakes that there is no way to cast off the burdens they now bear because of those sins. They feel weighted down by sorrow and despair, with no hope of escape.

Kristen and all of us should remember that while we are commanded to love God, he has a *perfect* love for us. All the world needs to be taught of the great redeeming power of the Savior's love. He loves us so much that he has promised to forgive us of those things we do that are wrong and remember them no more if we will only repent and come unto him. (See D&C 58:42.) He loves us so much that he was willing to pay the price for those sins. He suffered for us. He died for us. He said, Come follow me; cast your burdens on the Lord. His desire is to lift us, to help us, to guide us, to save us.

Some time ago someone gave me a gift. As I unwrapped the handsome package and discovered its contents, I was overcome with emotion. It was a precious item. I had seen it before in the office of the one who was now giving it to me. I had openly admired it for its unique capabilities and usefulness. It was finely crafted and very expensive. I was deeply touched as I received this generous gift—not because of its monetary value, but because I recognized the great love that the giving of this gift demonstrated to me. Here was an object I knew my benefactor could not afford to purchase for himself or for me. I knew that someone who loved him had bestowed that gift upon him and that he had been built up and made happy because of that gesture of love. Now in his desire to bring me happiness, to express his love to me, he was sharing one of the finest material possessions he had.

How grateful I am for this example of Christlike love and

for the many other gifts of love I experience daily in my home and in my associations throughout the Church. These experiences lift me up and give me the desire to extend my love to others.

May we as members of The Church of Jesus Christ of Latter-day Saints remember and live the first great commandments. May we each love the Lord with all our heart, all our soul, all our mind and strength, and may we love our neighbors as ourselves. May we show that love by living all the commandments of God and by sharing with our neighbors our greatest gift of love, the gospel of Jesus Christ.

Elder Robert L. Backman

"AS I HAVE LOVED YOU"

Fern attended high school in a small town. She was one of those nice but unnoticed girls who don't become much more than a face on a yearbook page and a name on the rolls. Her family was poor, and they lived out of town. She was not part of the "in crowd," and the only time her name came up in a conversation of other students was in that mocking, sarcastic way that seems funny when you are young, insecure, and need to ridicule someone else to take the pressure off yourself. Her name became synonymous with anything dumb or out of style. If a thing was unacceptable or ridiculous, the students called it "Ferny."

Young people can be so cruel.

It was an annual tradition in the school to recognize the student who showed the most school spirit and support for the athletic teams. On the day of the assembly to honor that student, as expected, they called out the name of one of the more popular girls in the school. She bounced up the aisle, smiling and waving to all her friends. But then a miracle happened. As she took the stage, she said, "I can't accept this award. Yes, I have loved the teams and cheered for them at every game. But Fern has come to every game too. I came in a nice, warm car surrounded by my happy friends. She came alone and walked all the way—two and a half miles—sometimes in the rain or

77

snow. She had to sit by herself, but I don't know anyone who cheered with as much spirit as Fern. I would like to nominate her for the most enthusiastic student in the school." Fern was escorted to the stage to a spontaneous standing ovation from her fellow students.

Youth can be so kind.

Fern is a mature woman today, her hair streaked with gray. Many things have happened to shape her life, but nothing more important than that outburst of acceptance and appreciation from her peers on that memorable day.

And there are mature men and women today who can't remember how many games their teams won or lost that year, but who have never forgotten the warm feeling they had when they stood up and cheered for Fern and welcomed her into their friendship and society.

Marianne Mortensen, a lovely Laurel in the Lancaster California Stake, told this story in a stake conference talk on the theme of showing charity toward our peers.

Reaching out to others is not an easy thing to do, particularly when you are young. To take the hand of another at the risk of your own popularity takes a mature, Christlike love. Yet our Savior made no distinction between young and old when he declared, "As I have loved you, . . . love one another." (John 13:34.) How desperately we need that kind of caring in our world today!

Young people are being hit on all sides by open and subtle attacks on their faith, their ideals, their morality, their self-confidence, even their identity. The typical teenager is pictured as being of the "Me" generation: self-centered, turned inward, unfeeling toward others, seeking immediate self-gratification. Though some young people might fit that description, and many are struggling and failing in the battle of life, others are winning in spectacular ways. Young men and women are accomplishing things today that we used to assume it took a lifetime to do. In science, literature, the arts, social, civic, and spiritual work, we can point with pride to millions of talented teenagers who have set lofty goals and are working to attain them. The question is, How can we help those who are stumbling to lock arms with those who are striding confidently up the road of life?

"Positive peer pressure," as the social scientists call it, may be the salvation of this generation. If this be true, think how admirably suited our Aaronic Priesthood quorums and our Young Women classes are to offer such meaningful service.

In her talk, Marianne Mortensen said: "Most of us have a difficult time resisting those who have a genuine love for us. Such people have a way of becoming important to us because we know we are genuinely important to them. The cry of youth today is for genuine concern and for meaningful relationships with our peers. . . . And when I speak of meaningful relationships, I think immediately of the Golden Rule, 'Do unto others as you would have them do unto you.' For teenagers, that is a difficult thing to do. Charity for those outside our circle of friends is difficult to comprehend when we feel so comfortable within the confines of our 'group.' But if we look at the life of our Savior, we see that he didn't leave his 'group,' the apostles, or those friends about him. He merely opened his arms to all who would listen. He increased his fold. So . . . we do not have to leave our group to learn to care for the feelings of our peers. We just need to open our arms and increase our friendships."

Marianne Mortensen was right on target.

There is another side to this matter of rendering service to others, not just to our peers, and it applies to those of us who are struggling to find our way.

As a boy I sought happiness as the world measures it. I wanted acceptance, position, fame (particularly as an athlete), and wealth. I had none of these. I was very unhappy. I thought happiness was as elusive as a shadow. It was not until I was called on a mission that I discovered the real key to happiness. To my surprise, despite the discouragement, the disappointments, and the plain hard work associated with my missionary labors, I was happy. It was then that I learned that happiness is really a by-product of service. As I forgot my own desires, my own weaknesses and frailties in my missionary service, I began to understand King Benjamin's profound counsel to his people: "Behold, I tell you these things that ye may learn wisdom; that ye may learn that when ye are in the service of your fellow beings ye are only in the service of your God." (Mosiah 2:17.) That is why a missionary can return from the toughest experiences of his life and report, "These have been the happiest two years of my life!"

A life can never be happy that is focused inward. So if you are miserable now, forget your troubles. March right out your door, and find someone who needs you. You want happiness? Find ways to serve. Your happiness will be commensurate with the service you render. Just think how much that joy can grow as we expand our love and service to more and more people. Consider the happiness generated in both the giver and the receiver by these examples of service:

1. Youths of the Meridian Idaho East Stake participated in a community-wide "Paint Your Heart Out" service project. One hundred and sixty-four youths split into five teams, and each team painted one house of an elderly person during a seven-hour period.

2. Concerned for the youth of his ward, a good bishop in Bountiful, Utah, challenged them to taste the sweetness of beautiful service. Reluctantly at first, they put aside their entertainment. One project was making quilts for the mentally retarded at the American Fork Training School. Upon completion of their quilts, the young women delivered them. They arrived at the school in time to help feed supper to the residents of the school. And that was an experience. As they left the school, with mashed potatoes, gravy, and assorted vegetables in their hair and on their outfits, one young woman, touched by the sweetness of the person she had fed, said, "I'll never forget Billy."

3. In a recent letter to the editor, I read: "One is continually hearing about the 'Terrible Teenagers' with their obnoxious dress and deplorable actions. How refreshing it was to have a most thrilling experience with—yes, four teenagers.

"One evening I was hosting a special guest from New York City. We were on our beautiful Temple Square, admiring the Seagull Monument. As we turned to go, four teenagers approached us. I immediately felt the [in]security of my gentleman guest, when one of the group stepped forward and said, 'Lady, we would like to present you with this rose to make you happy, and hope that you will have a nice evening.' There clutched in his hand was a beautiful, long-stemmed American Beauty red rose, with a spray of fern, artistically wrapped in cellophane. 'We bought this rose to give to someone, and when we saw you, we thought you were the one.'

"As they turned to leave, I quickly got their names, expressing my most profound appreciation and admiration for their thoughtfulness and kindness to me, which was so unusual, and how I was quite overwhelmed to think that four teenagers would have the desire for such a gracious act, and that no one would appreciate it more than I would, a little grandmother, as I gave each one a big hug." (Irene E. Staples, *Deseret News,* Sept. 22, 1985.)

4. With the knowledge that her little brother had leukemia, Michelle went to Bear River (Utah) High School sad and despondent. She struggled through the school day, grateful when the dismissal bell rang. As she collected her books, a friend approached and said, "Michelle, come into the music room with me." Half-heartedly, Michelle accompanied her. Entering the music room, she was surprised to find the entire a cappella choir. In the straightforward manner of youth, they told Michelle they had been fasting for her little brother and wanted her to join them as they prayed together to end their fast.

Emerson said it well: "Serve, and thou shalt be served. If you love and serve men, you cannot, by any hiding or stratagem, escape the remuneration."

Those we serve, we love. We discover that loving someone else deeply is one of the most joyous feelings we can know, and we begin to understand the bounteous love our Father in heaven has for us.

D. Brent Collette told a stirring story:

"Ronny was not just shy; he was downright backward. As a 17-year-old high school senior, Ronny had never really had a close friend or done anything that included other people. He was famous for his shyness. He never said anything to anybody, not even a teacher. One look at him told you a great deal of the story—inferiority complex. He slumped over as if to hide his face and seemed to be always looking at his feet. He always sat in the back of the class and would never participate. . . .

"It was because of Ronny's shyness that I was so astonished when he started coming to my Sunday School class. . . . His attendance in my class was the result of the personal efforts of a classmate, Brandon Craig, who had recently befriended Ronny. Boy, if there had ever been a mismatch, this was it. Brandon was 'Mr. Social.' A good head taller than Ronny, he was undisputedly the number one star of our high school athletics program. Brandon was involved in everything and successful at every-thing. . . . He was just a neat boy.

"Well, Brandon took to little Ronny like glue. Class was obviously painful for Ronny, but Brandon protected him like the king's guard. I played a low profile—no questions, just a quick smile and once a pat on the back. Time seemed to be helping, but I often wondered if Brandon and company (the rest of the class certainly played it right) would ever be able to break the ice. That's why I was so shocked when Brian, the class president, stood before our Sunday School class one Sunday afternoon and boldly announced that Ronny would offer the opening prayer.

"There was a moment of hesitation; then Ronny slowly came to his feet. Still looking at his shoes, he walked to the front of the room. He folded his arms (his head was already bowed). The class was frozen solid. I thought to myself, 'If he does it, we'll all be translated.' Then almost at a whisper I heard, 'Our Father in heaven, thank you for our Sunday School class.' Then silence—long, loud silence! I could feel poor Ronny suffering. Then came a few sniffles and a muffled sob.

"'Oh, no,' I thought, 'I should be up front where I can help or something.' I hurt for him; we all did. I opened an eye and looked up to make my way to Ronny. But Brandon beat me to it. With an eye still open I watched six-foot-four Brandon put his arm around his friend, bend down and put his chin on Ronny's shoulder, then whisper the words of a short, sweet prayer. Ronny struggled for composure, then repeated the prayer.

"But when the prayer was over, Ronny kept his head bowed and added: 'Thank you for Brandon. Amen.' He then turned and looked up at this big buddy and said, clear enough for all to hear, 'I love you, Brandon.'

"Brandon, who still had his arm around him, responded, 'I love you too, Ronny. And that was fun.'

"And it was, for all of us." (*New Era,* May 1983, p. 18.)

Our Primary children sing that glorious song:

> *As I have loved you, love one another,*
> *This new commandment: Love one another.*
> *By this shall men know ye are my disciples,*
> *If ye have love one to another.*
> *(Hymns,* 1985, no. 308.)

And therein lies happiness.

Elder Robert E. Wells

THE LOVE BANK: A FABLE

Once upon a time there was a banker. He was a good, thoughtful man, and, like most bankers, he was thinking about that which is close to the heart of all bankers: the interest rate. If you were to ask this banker to list the greatest inventions of all time in order of their importance to mankind, he would unhesitatingly rank the charging of interest as the most important of all, even above electricity, the steam engine, atomic power, and so on.

You see, if you lend money at interest, you hardly have to work to make a profit. You need only to make wise decisions as to whom you can trust to return the money at the appointed time with the agreed interest. The banker keeps the interest for himself, his employees, and his patrons and turns around to loan the same money out again. It is a nice business. Everyone seems to come out ahead. The person who puts his money in the bank as savings can get more money back than he deposited at any time he wants it back. The person who borrows makes a profit on his business transaction, so he is happy to split that profit by returning more to the bank than he borrowed. So our thoughtful banker was happily meditating upon this miraculous circle of mutual benefits to the depositer, the borrower, and, of course, the banker.

Then he remembered that the Savior had good things to say

about interest too. He turned to the parable of the talents in Matthew. This parable tells of a servant who took his master's five talents and traded them until he had doubled the money. The second servant took his two talents and did likewise. But the third servant did not use the money; he hid it so as not to lose it, earning nothing with it. When the master returned and asked for an accounting, he commended both the first and the second servants equally for having been faithful. He promised them increased responsibilities in the future, with implied higher benefits for them. He scolded the third, called him slothful, and said, "Thou oughtest therefore to have put my money to the exchangers [the bankers of that day], and then at my coming I should have received mine own with usury [what we call interest]." (Matthew 25:27.) The banker realized that the Savior did know the advantage of interest.

He then thought of the several different kinds of banks: money banks, blood banks, eye cornea banks, and royal jelly banks. Why not have a love bank! He quickly organized and opened the new love bank in his city. Anyone depositing acts of love would receive more in return when they withdrew them. The only restriction was that those who borrowed love could not use it for themselves but had to give the love to someone else. The love bank grew and prospered with all the increased love.

A father borrowed some love from the bank and gave it to his children. He was amazed at what happened. Not only did he receive blessings in his relationship with his children, but it also seemed as though he suddenly received more love from others: his wife, his parents, his neighbors, his quorum president, and his fellow workers.

A wife borrowed some love from the bank and used it on her husband. With the loan, she gave much more love and affection than ever before. The more she did for her husband, the more she loved him, and the more he returned that love. The children noticed how much love mom gave dad, and they too gave dad and mom more attention, more obedience, and more love. The wife became such a happy person that love just came to her from all sides. The Relief Society work went better. The sisters gave her more love than ever before. The grouchy neighbor changed into a person happy to see her, loving her as a sister. Her mother-in-law, seeing such a loving family, changed her mind and said that her son had made a wise choice in his marriage. The children also found that they could borrow love from the bank. They gave love to each other. Astounding results! There was no more rivalry or quarreling. They shared happily. They willingly completed their assigned chores and did extra things.

The borrowing families had so much love left over after paying back their loan at the bank, with interest, that they didn't have any place for all the extra love. Just as we share our surplus from our gardens with neighbors and friends, they began to share the surplus love with their neighbors and friends. They ran errands, tended children, mowed lawns for vacationers, and helped those who were ill. They made phantom cookie deliveries and performed phantom car washes while no one was looking. The blessings they received in return were greater if no one knew who had done it.

This made the surplus of love grow even more. It was unbelievable! The friendshiping and the fellowshiping just wouldn't stop. The only thing left was to share and teach the gospel to everyone. They bore testimony of the influence of the gospel of love in their lives. They told about Christ and his miracles of love. They asked the golden questions. They loaned the Book of Mormon. They brought friends to church. They took them to baptismal services. They invited the missionaries into their homes for group discussions. They became missionaries all day long and were examples of unselfish love in action.

Do you know what happened? The people were full of love; the city was full of love; the bank was full of love. They had discovered the secret!

I have it from a good source—the bank and the banker really did exist. But I have searched all over the world and can't find them anywhere, so they must have gone where Enoch and his city went.

Each one of us is a banker of love. We have great resources and treasures of love stored away in our banks. In addition, each of us has an unlimited source of love to draw on—the

Savior. Now we just have to get our love out and put it in circulation. That is when it starts multiplying. Unlike bank regulations, there is no ceiling on the loans of love you may place. There is no reserve requirement. You don't have to keep a part of it in reserve. The only regulation is that you do each loving act and expect nothing in return. Do everything possible so that the beneficiary will not know you, nor can he repay you. Cast your bread upon the waters of life.

Remember, love "suffereth long, and is kind, and envieth not, and is not puffed up, seeketh not her own, is not easily provoked, thinketh no evil, and . . . rejoiceth in the truth, beareth all things, believeth all things, hopeth all things, endureth all things." (Moroni 7:45.)

Elder Ronald E. Poelman

GOD'S LOVE FOR US TRANSCENDS OUR TRANSGRESSIONS

The Galilean fisherman Simon Peter, upon recognizing for the first time the divine power of Jesus, exclaimed, "Depart from me; for I am a sinful man, O Lord." (Luke 5:8.)

Each one of us, at times, may feel like Peter, conscious of our failings and uncomfortable at the thought of approaching the Lord. Transgression causes us to feel estranged from our Father in heaven, and we feel unworthy of his love and fearful of his disapproval. Yet, having transgressed his laws or disobeyed his commandments, we need the strengthening influence of our Father to help us overcome our weakness, to help us repent and become reconciled with him. Unrepented sin tends to become habitual and is frequently accompanied by a deepening sense of guilt, which may make repentance increasingly difficult. This feeling of estrangement from the Lord becomes an impediment to repentance and reconciliation with him.

Knowing we have offended our Father in heaven, we are afraid to ask his help, feeling that we don't deserve it. Paradoxically, when we are most in need of the Lord's influence, we deserve it least. Nevertheless, in such circumstances he says to us, as Jesus said to the trembling Peter, "Fear not." (Luke 5:10.)

My message might best be illustrated through the experiences of a young couple whom I will call John and Gayle. John was a thoughtful, kind young man, affectionate, with a frank and open manner. He sincerely tried to obey the Lord's commandments and found honest contentment in the joys of family life. Gayle, his wife, was young, attractive, high-spirited, but inclined toward more worldly interests and activities. The society in which they lived was, in general, one of affluence and materialism. People seemed preoccupied with temporal gain, social status, entertainment, and self-gratification. Religious leaders were concerned about the apparent breakdown in family life and moral standards.

In the early years of their marriage, John and Gayle were blessed with children, first a boy and then a girl; but Gayle seemed uninterested in her domestic responsibilities. She longed for glamour and excitement in her life and was frequently away from home at parties and entertainments, not always with her husband. In her vanity, Gayle encouraged and responded to the attentions of other men until eventually she was unfaithful to her marriage vows.

Throughout, John encouraged Gayle to appreciate the joys of family life and experience the rewards of observing the laws of God. He was patient and kind, but to no avail. Shortly after the birth of a third child, a son, Gayle deserted her husband and children and joined her worldly friends in a life of self-indulgence and immorality. John, thus rejected, was humiliated and brokenhearted.

Soon, however, the glamour and excitement that had attracted Gayle turned to ashes. Her so-called friends tired of her and abandoned her. Then each successive step was downward, her life becoming more and more degraded. Eventually she recognized her mistakes and realized what she had lost, but she could see no way back. Certainly John could not possibly love her still. She felt completely unworthy of his love and undeserving of her home and family.

Then one day, passing through the streets, John recognized Gayle. Surely he would have been justified in turning away, but he didn't. As he observed the effects of her recent life, all too evident, a feeling of compassion came over him—a desire to reach out to her. Learning that Gayle had incurred substantial debts, John repaid them and then took her home.

Soon John realized, at first with amazement, that he still loved Gayle. Out of his love for her and her willingness to change and begin anew, there grew in his heart a feeling of merciful forgiveness, a desire to help her overcome her past and to accept her again fully as his wife.

Through his personal experience there arose in John another profound awareness, a realization of the nature of God's love for us, his children. Though we disregard his counsel, break his commandments, and reject him, when we recognize our mistakes and desire to repent, he wants us to seek him out and he will accept us. John had been prepared, through his personal experiences, for a divine mission. Though I have taken some literary license in telling the story, it is the account, perhaps allegorical, of Hosea, prophet of the Old Testament, and his wife, Gomer.

Portraying God to ancient Israel as a loving, forgiving father, Hosea foreshadowed, more than most Old Testament prophets, the spirit and message of the New Testament, the Book of Mormon, and modern revelation.

In these latter days the Lord has said: "For I the Lord cannot look upon sin with the least degree of allowance; nevertheless, he that repents and does the commandments of the Lord shall be forgiven." (D&C 1:31-32.) By disobeying the laws of God and breaking his commandments, we do offend him, we do estrange ourselves from him, and we don't deserve his help and inspiration and strength. But God's love for us transcends our transgressions.

When we disobey the laws of God, justice requires that compensation be made—a requirement that we are incapable of fulfilling. But out of his divine love for us, our Father has provided a plan and a Savior, Jesus Christ, whose redeeming sacrifice satisfies the demands of justice for us and makes possible repentance, forgiveness, and reconciliation with our Father. For indeed, "God so loved the world, that he gave his only begotten Son, that whosoever believeth in him should not perish, but have everlasting life." (John 3:16.)

We may accept this great gift through faith in Jesus Christ

and repentance, followed by a covenant made with him through baptism of the water and of the Spirit. Then, each week, as we receive the sacrament, we renew our covenant that we will "always remember him and keep his commandments." The promise attached to that covenant is that we "may always have his Spirit to be with [us]." (D&C 20:77.)

Hosea's ancient message is repeated and elaborated throughout the scriptures. Through Isaiah, another Old Testament prophet, the Lord said to his people: "Wash you, make you clean; put away the evil of your doings from before mine eyes; cease to do evil; learn to do well. . . . Come now, and let us reason together, saith the Lord: though your sins be as scarlet, they shall be as white as snow; though they be red like crimson, they shall be as wool." (Isaiah 1:16-18.)

The Lord, speaking to Alma, the Nephite prophet, says: "Whosoever transgresseth against me, him shall ye judge according to the sins which he has committed; and if he confess his sins before thee and me, and repenteth in the sincerity of his heart, him shall ye forgive, and I will forgive him also. Yea, and as often as my people repent will I forgive them their trespasses against me." (Mosiah 26:29-30.)

Too often we make repentance more difficult for each other by our failure to forgive one another. However, we are admonished in modern revelation that "ye ought to forgive one another; for he that forgiveth not his brother his trespasses standeth condemned before the Lord; for there remaineth in him the greater sin. I, the Lord, will forgive whom I will forgive, but of you it is required to forgive all men." (D&C 64:9-10.)

Also from modern revelation comes one of the most comforting, hopeful pronouncements ever spoken: "He who has repented of his sins, the same is forgiven, and I, the Lord, remember them no more." (D&C 58:42.)

God is our Father; he loves us; his love is infinite and unconditional. His sorrow is great when we disobey his commandments and break his laws. He cannot condone our transgressions, but he loves us and wants us to return to him. I know of no greater inducement to repentance and reconciliation with him than an awareness of his love for us personally and individually.

Elder Marion D. Hanks

FORGIVENESS: THE ULTIMATE FORM OF LOVE

After a meeting with a group of students, one young man waited to ask a question. "Elder Hanks," he said, "what are *your* goals? What do *you* want to accomplish?" I observed his seriousness of purpose and answered in the same spirit that my strongest desire is to qualify to be a friend of Christ. I had not responded to such a question just that way before, but the answer did put into words the deep yearnings of my heart.

In ancient times Abraham was called the "friend of God." Jesus, shortly before his crucifixion, said to his disciples, "Ye are my friends, if ye do whatsoever I command you. Henceforth I call you not servants . . . but I have called you friends." (John 15:14-15.) In 1832, to a group of elders returning from missionary service, he repeated the message: "From henceforth I shall call you friends." (D&C 84:77.)

Christ's love was so pure that he gave his life for us: "Greater love hath no man than this, that a man lay down his life for his friends." (John 15:13.) But there was another gift he bestowed while he was on the cross, a gift that further measured the magnitude of his great love: he forgave, and he asked his

Father to forgive, those who persecuted and crucified him.

Was this act of forgiveness less difficult than sacrificing his mortal life? Was it less a test of his love? I do not know the answer. But I have felt that the ultimate form of love for God and men is forgiveness. He met the test. What of us? Perhaps we shall not be called upon to give our lives for our friends or our faith (though perhaps some shall), but it is certain that everyone has had and will have occasion to confront the other challenge. What will we do with it? What *are* we doing with it?

Someone has written: "The withholding of love is the negation of the spirit of Christ, the proof that we never knew him, that for us he lived in vain. It means that he suggested nothing in all our thoughts, that he inspired nothing in all our lives, that we were not once near enough to him to be seized with the spell of his compassion for the world." Christ's example and instructions to his friends are clear. He forgave, and he said: "Love your enemies, bless them that curse you, do good to them that hate you, and pray for them which despitefully use you, and persecute you." (Matthew 5:44.)

What is our response when we are offended, misunderstood, unfairly or unkindly treated, or sinned against, made an offender for a word, falsely accused, passed over, hurt by those we love, our offerings rejected? Do we resent, become bitter, hold a grudge? Or do we resolve the problem if we can, forgive, and rid ourselves of the burden? The nature of our response to such situations may well determine the nature and quality of our lives, here and eternally. A courageous friend, her faith refined by many afflictions, said to me some time ago, "Humiliation must come before exaltation."

It is required of us to forgive. Our salvation depends upon it. In a revelation given in 1831 the Lord said: "My disciples, in days of old, sought occasion against one another and forgave not one another in their hearts; and for this evil they were afflicted and sorely chastened. Wherefore, I say unto you, that ye ought to forgive one another: for he that forgiveth not his brother his trespasses standeth condemned before the Lord: for there remaineth in him the greater sin. I, the Lord, will forgive whom I will forgive, but of you it is required to forgive all men." (D&C 64:8-10.) Therefore, Jesus taught us to pray:

"And forgive us our trespasses as we forgive those who trespass against us." (Matthew 6: 14-15.)

Does it not seem a supreme impudence to ask and expect God to forgive when we do not forgive?—openly? and "in our hearts"? The Lord affirms in the Book of Mormon that we bring ourselves under condemnation if we do not forgive. (See Mosiah 26:30-31.)

Not just our eternal salvation depends upon our willingness and capacity to forgive wrongs committed against us. In addition, our joy and satisfaction in this life, and our true freedom, depend upon our doing so. When Christ bade us turn the other cheek, walk the second mile, give our cloak to him who takes our coat, was it to be chiefly out of consideration for the bully, the brute, the thief? Or was it to relieve the one aggrieved of the destructive burden that resentment and anger lay upon us?

Paul wrote to the Romans that nothing "shall be able to separate us from the love of God, which is in Christ Jesus our Lord." (Romans 8:39.) I am sure that this is true. I bear testimony that this is true. But it is also true that we can *separate ourselves* from his spirit. In Isaiah it is written: "Your iniquities have separated between you and your God." (Isaiah 59:2.) Again, "They have rewarded evil unto themselves." (Isaiah 3:9.) Through Helaman we learn that "whosoever doeth iniquity, doeth it unto himself" (Helaman 14:30); and from Benjamin, "Ye do withdraw yourselves from the Spirit of the Lord" (Mosiah 2:36).

In every case of sin this is true. Envy, arrogance, unrighteous dominion—these canker the soul of one who is guilty of them. It is true also if we fail to forgive. Even if it appears that another may be deserving of our resentment or hatred, none of us can afford to pay the price of resenting or hating because of what it does to us. If we have felt the gnawing, mordant inroads of these emotions, we know the harm we suffer. So Paul taught the Corinthians that they must "see that none render evil for evil unto any man." (1 Thessalonians 5:15).

It is reported that President Brigham Young once said that he who takes offense when no offense was intended is a fool, and he who takes offense when offense *was* intended is usually a fool. It was then explained that there are two courses of action to follow when one is bitten by a rattlesnake. One may, in anger, fear, or vengefulness, pursue the creature and kill it. Or he may make full haste to get the venom out of his system. If we pursue the latter course, we will likely survive, but if we attempt to follow the former, we may not be around long enough to finish what we started.

Years ago on Temple Square I heard a boy pour out the anguish of his troubled heart and make a commitment to God. He had been living in a spirit of hatred toward a man who had criminally taken the life of his father. Nearly bereft of his senses with grief, he had been overcome with bitterness. On that Sabbath morning when others and I heard him, he had been touched by the Spirit of the Lord, and in that hour, through the pouring in of that spirit, the hostility that had filled his heart had flooded out. He tearfully declared his determined intent to leave vengeance to the Lord and justice to the law. He would no longer hate the one who had caused the grievous loss. He would forgive and would not for another hour permit the corrosive spirit of vengefulness to fill his heart.

Some time later, touched with the remembrance of that moving Sabbath morning, I told the story to a group of people in another city. Before I left that small community the next day, I was visited by a man who had heard the message and understood it. Later a letter came from him. He had gone home that night and prayed and prepared himself and had then visited the place of a man in his community who had years before imposed upon the sanctity of his home. There had been animosity and revenge in his heart and threats made. That evening when it was made known that he was at the door, his frightened neighbor appeared with a weapon in his hand. The man quickly explained the reasons for his visit, that he had come to say that he was sorry, that he did not want hatred to continue to consume his life. He offered forgiveness and sought forgiveness and went his way in tears, a free man for the first time in years. He left a former adversary also in tears, shaken and repentant.

The next day the same man went to the home of a relative in the town. He said, "I came to ask your forgiveness. I don't even remember why we have been angry so long, but I have come to tell you that I am sorry and to beg your pardon and to say that I have learned how foolish I have been." He was invited in to join the family at their table, and was reunited with his kin.

When I heard his story, I knew again the importance of qualifying ourselves for the forgiveness of Christ by forgiving.

Robert Louis Stevenson wrote: "The truth of Christ's teaching seems to be this: In our own person and fortune, we should be ready to accept and pardon all; it is our cheek we are to turn and our coat we are to give to the man who has taken our cloak. But when another's face is buffeted, perhaps a little of the lion will become us best. That we are to suffer others to be injured and stand by, is not conceivable and surely not desirable."

So there are times when, in defense of others and principle, we must act. But of ourselves, if we suffer injury or unkindness, we must pray for the strength to forbear. Christ gave his life on a cross; and on that cross he fully, freely forgave. It is a worthy goal to seek to qualify for the friendship of such a one.

More than 250 years ago Joseph Addison printed in *The Spectator* a paragraph of sobering thoughtfulness: "When I look upon the tombs of the great, every emotion of envy dies in me; when I read the epitaphs of the beautiful, every inordinate desire goes out; when I meet with the grief of parents upon a tombstone, my heart melts with compassion; when I see the tombs of the parents themselves, I consider the vanity of grieving for those whom we must quickly follow; when I see kings lying by those who deposed them, when I consider rival wits placed side by side, or the men that divided the world with their contests and disputes, I reflect with sorrow and astonishment on the little competitions, factions, and debates of mankind. When I read the several dates of the tombs, of some that died yesterday, and some six hundred years ago; I consider that great Day when we shall all of us be contemporaries, and make our appearance together."

God help us to rid ourselves of resentment and pettiness and foolish pride, to love, and to forgive, in order that we may be friends with ourselves, with others, and with the Lord.

INDEX